Simplicity

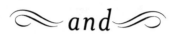 *and*

Excellence

Simplicity
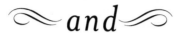 *and*

Excellence

ELIZABETH KREMER

from Beaten Biscuits *to*
Shaker Lemon Pie

DEIRDRE A. SCAGGS AND
EVALINA KREMER SETTLE

Foreword by Ouita Michel
Afterword by sara bradley

UNIVERSITY PRESS OF KENTUCKY

Copyright © 2024 by The University Press of Kentucky

Scholarly publisher for the Commonwealth,
serving Bellarmine University, Berea College, Centre College of Kentucky,
Eastern Kentucky University, The Filson Historical Society, Georgetown
College, Kentucky Historical Society, Kentucky State University, Morehead
State University, Murray State University, Northern Kentucky University,
Spalding University, Transylvania University, University of Kentucky,
University of Louisville, University of Pikeville, and Western Kentucky
University.

Editorial and Sales Offices: The University Press of Kentucky
663 South Limestone Street, Lexington, Kentucky 40508-4008
www.kentuckypress.com

Cataloging-in-Publication data available from the Library of Congress

ISBN 978-0-8131-9934-4 (hardcover)
ISBN 978-1-9859-0004-2 (paperback)
ISBN 978-1-9859-0006-6 (pdf)
ISBN 978-1-9859-0007-3 (epub)

This book is printed on acid-free paper meeting
the requirements of the American National Standard
for Permanence in Paper for Printed Library Materials.

Manufactured in the United States of America.

Member of the Association of
University Presses

A woman must work twice as hard as a man
for half the recognition.
—Elizabeth Kremer

This book is dedicated to all those women.

Contents

Foreword   ix

Preface   xiii

1. A Sense of Place   1

2. The College Student   23

3. The Professional   51

4. The Home Economist   101

5. Shaker Your Plate   161

Epilogue   209

Afterword   211

Acknowledgments   213

Selected Resources   215

Index of Recipes   217

Foreword

Elizabeth Kremer's professional story is so similar to my own. The recipes she prepared nearly a century ago still grace the pages of menus I write today, as I'm always looking for that authentic flavor of Kentucky.

We both graduated from the University of Kentucky and ventured to New York City in our early twenties to begin long careers in restaurant management. Her books, *We Make You Kindly Welcome: Recipes from the Trustees' House Daily Fare* and *Welcome Back to Pleasant Hill: More Recipes from the Trustees' House*, are well-worn entries in my personal culinary library.

Shakertown has long been special to me; although I never met Mrs. Kremer, her dining room there was so memorable that it inspired in me, at a very early age, a deep love and regard for restaurants. She paved the way and set me on my own Kentucky restaurant path.

It was riveting to read this biography, started by her daughter Evalina Kremer Settle and completed and brought to life by Deirdre A. Scaggs. Each chapter of Elizabeth Kremer's life is told through stories seasoned with wonderful recipes. There are buckwheat pancakes, Chan Tart, broiled quail with cream gravy, and beaten biscuits from her childhood in Cynthiana.

A few months living in California yielded a delicious ambrosia recipe. Arroz con pollo and gazpacho were the reward for a stint teaching on sugar plantations in Cuba while she earned enough money to attend the University of Kentucky.

There's a treasure trove of candy recipes: divinity, candy pudding, seafoam, chocolate fudge, and the famous Modjeskas—all made with other girls in the kitchen of the University of Kentucky's Patterson Hall dorm during the early 1920s. There are gems from Mrs. Jewell's Tea Room and teas held at Maxwell Place by Mrs. Frances Jewell McVey. But it wasn't all fun and games at the university. In those days, earning a home economics degree from the College of Agriculture required learning how to kill a chicken, clean it, dress it, and cut it up for frying!

The restaurant details of Elizabeth's early professional life are wonderful: her work as a "salad girl" at Schrafft's in New York City, the description of the French Village in Louisville, reopening after the great flood of 1937. At the Canary Cottage, Elizabeth held the food cost to 2 percent of sales, an amazing testament to just how granular her scratch-cooking really was. In 1937, the cottage recorded $207,266.84 in sales and served 324,783 guests, for a check average of 63¢—pretty good value for such legendary dishes as fried soft-shell crabs, pot roast, oyster stew, and even oysters Rockefeller!

During a time when women were just a small percentage of the workforce, Elizabeth managed multiple very successful restaurants in New York City, Louisville, and Cincinnati, serving hundreds of thousands of customers every year—through Prohibition and the Great Depression. When alcohol sales became legal again, she promptly researched the new liquor laws and trained her staff to make cocktails. It is fascinating and inspiring to read her restaurant recipes, points of service, and dining room philosophy—much of it still timely more than ninety years later.

In March 1935, having been introduced by mutual friends Cissy and Ed Gregg, Elizabeth married Harold "Doc" Pemberton Kremer. She continued to lead the Canary Cottage in Cincinnati, while he lived and worked in Louisville. Even after their first daughter, Pem, was born, she continued running the restaurant. It wasn't until late into her second pregnancy that she paused her professional life to raise their two daughters in Louisville.

At the age of sixty-five, after Doc Kremer's death, Mrs. Kremer was recruited out of her long retirement to open the dining room in the Trustees' Office (it was historically called the Trustees' House) at Shakertown, one of my favorite places in Kentucky to visit and dine at, and once one of our state's truest and most authentic expressions of Kentucky hospitality, a bastion of Kentucky food culture and history.

Mrs. Kremer started out with a small soup-and-sandwich counter in the Old Stone Shop during the summer of 1967 while village restoration was underway. She designed the kitchen for the Trustees' Office and actively helped research appropriate uniforms, menu style, and authentic Shaker recipes; she even inspired the kitchen garden. Reading the details of her dining room service brought it back to life for me. I can so clearly remember the flickering candles in their tall glass hurricanes, the big wooden bowls of cut vegetables, baskets of rolls and corn sticks, and even the white aprons and little white hats worn by the ladies serving in the dining room. I loved the fried chicken and the passed platters of side dishes. And Shaker lemon pie is still one of my all-time favorite desserts.

In 2015, I was honored to be a guest chef at Shakertown and to cook a dinner featuring the recipes of my friend Rona Roberts, who wrote *Classic Kentucky Meals*. It was served outside under a full moon, next to the kitchen garden. I'd like to think Mrs. Kremer was there in spirit. Thank you, Deirdre, for protecting and adding to her legacy and publishing this book so that we may all embrace the amazing life and work of Elizabeth Kremer.

Ouita Michel, Chef
Owner of Holly Hill Inn, Wallace Station Deli,
Windy Corner Market, Smithtown Seafood,
Honeywood, and Zim's Café
Author of *Just a Few Miles South:
Timeless Recipes from Our
Favorite Places*

Preface

In 2016, I met Evalina Kremer Settle at Frances Jewell Hammond's home, Pleasant View Farm, 9588 Harrodsburg Road, Jessamine County, Kentucky. Frances lived in the former country home of her grandparents, Lizzie and Asa Jewell, the site of Jewell's Tea Room, a restaurant that makes an important appearance later in this book. That day, Evalina wanted to talk about additional family papers that she was interested in donating to the University of Kentucky Libraries Special Collections Research Center. Within those papers was a working manuscript about the life of Elizabeth Kremer, Evalina's mother. She told me that she was not going to be able to work toward publication and asked if I thought I could "do something with it." Evalina knew about my previous book, *The Historic Kentucky Kitchen*, and I am so grateful that she trusted me with her mother's story. In 2021, I was finally ready to follow through on my promise, and on October 18 of that year, I phoned Evalina and her husband John to say that I had signed a contract with the University Press of Kentucky. Coincidentally, I made that phone call on what would have been Elizabeth's 120th birthday.

Much of the original background for this project involved oral histories conducted by Elizabeth's daughters, Evalina and Pem, with their mother's friends and their children. Many of the stories came from family tales that were repeated over the years—most over the table at Christmas, Thanksgiving, birthday parties, and funeral gatherings. I complemented the family history with extensive archival research. Regarding the stories, should errors occur, the daughters invoked one of their mother's favorite sayings, "If it's not true, it ought to be!"

1

A Sense of Place

According to Sarah Swinford Kinney, one of Elizabeth's childhood friends, "Elizabeth had a strong sense of place. And that place was Cynthiana, Kentucky." Cynthiana, established in 1793, is a small town along the banks of the South Fork Licking River in Kentucky, located twenty-eight miles northeast of Lexington, Kentucky, and sixty miles south of Cincinnati, Ohio. In the early 1900s, Cynthiana was a prosperous community built on the success of burley tobacco farms and bourbon distilleries. Its population in 1900 was 3,257. Elizabeth Cromwell was born on October 18, 1901, in Cynthiana, Kentucky, to John and Evalina Cromwell.

Named after Eva's sister, Elizabeth "Lizzie" Berry, Elizabeth was the sixth of seven children born to Eva Goddard Berry, 1865–1929, from Berry Station in Harrison County, and John Morgan Cromwell, 1862–1951, of Cynthiana. Eva "Eva" Cromwell came from a family who valued shared meals and excellent cooks. As a result, the Cromwell family's meals were the epitome of Victorian elegance. The children—in birth order, Louise, Belle, Henry, Anna, Lillie, Elizabeth, and James—helped with the food service, and dining was a time for the family to gather and discuss the day's plans or events. Proper table manners were expected from every child present, regardless of age.

The *White House Cook Book*, by F. L. Gillette, was passed down through the family since its first printing in 1887. The women in the family considered this cookbook to be the ultimate authority on not only meal preparation but also dining behavior and table manners. The instructions and advice in the *White House Cook Book* were the law of the land. This excerpt on table etiquette reflects that ideology:

> Delicacy of manner at table stamps both man and woman, for one can, at a glance, discern whether a person has been trained to eat well—i.e. to hold the knife and fork properly, to eat without the slightest sound of the lips, to drink quietly, to use the napkin rightly, to make no noise with any of the implements of the table, and last, but not least, to eat slowly and masticate the food thoroughly. All these points should be most carefully taught to children, and then they will always feel at their ease at the grandest tables in the land. There is no position where the innate refinement of a person is more fully exhibited than at the table, and nowhere that those who have not been trained in table etiquette feel more keenly their deficiencies.

The main meal at Eva's table was midday dinner, or lunch, as it is more commonly referred to today. As such, it was accompanied by a complete table service, and each day's midday meal was treated as a special event. There were rarely any leftovers, since the immediate family as well as friends and other relatives were usually in attendance at the long dining table. The elaborate meals and service were possible because of the family's cook and housekeeper. Like other women of her era, Eva employed a Black woman, whom the family called "Cuz." It was noted that Eva herself did not cook but oversaw the dining activities. Cuz was employed by the family through the birth and growth of all seven of the Cromwell children and of various pets. She continued with the Cromwell family

Cuz and Henry Cromwell, around 1900. This photograph was found pasted in John Cromwell's scrapbook, made in memory of his late son, Henry. University of Kentucky Libraries (UKL), John M. Cromwell Scrapbooks, 2014ms095.

through the early death of the third-oldest child, Henry, and the death of the family's matriarch, Eva. Cuz lived to see four grand-children come into the family. Despite the length of Cuz's employment, little documentation exists about her history or story. The 1930 census lists Emma Keller as the Cromwell's servant, so it is possible that this is Cuz's real name.

There are many family photographs where Elizabeth is pictured with animals, from ducks to cats! Here, young Elizabeth Kremer is holding her pet cat, and brother Jim is holding her beloved raccoon. UKL, Elizabeth Kremer Cromwell Papers, 2016ms043.

Elizabeth was a small girl who was loving, wistful, mischievous, occasionally frightened, often unexpectedly bold, and always innovative. The family kitchen fascinated young Elizabeth, and she spent a great deal of time with Cuz in that kitchen. She dearly loved Cuz, though this affection did not stop Elizabeth's mischievous nature. Elizabeth recalled, not altogether penitently, that she used to let her pet raccoon into the kitchen to tease Cuz, who was very afraid of the animal. Elizabeth had a long succession of pets, including several cats that she named after her sister's boyfriends, a goose, and her raccoon. The raccoon seemed to have been her favorite, and she grieved that it never returned from its second hibernation.

Weekends were opportunities for more special meals. Buckwheat cakes or pancakes were part of Saturday morning special breakfasts that often included sausage, biscuits, and orange marmalade. Elizabeth would regularly slip into Cuz's kitchen, where she could spend time with the woman and learn more about the kitchen. She fondly recalled the Saturday mornings when special breakfasts were made and that Cuz would teach her how to make the weekend treats, especially orange marmalade. Elizabeth's sister, Louise, kept a handwritten book with family recipes, and I speculate that many of those handwritten recipes were based on meals that Cuz prepared.

Buckwheat Cakes

1 cup of buckwheat flour
1 cup of flour
2 tablespoons of molasses
1 egg
4 teaspoons B. P.
1 teaspoon of salt
1¾ cup of sweet milk

Sift flours, salt, B. P. together
Beat whole egg and beat
milk in egg with Dover egg
beater. Add molasses gradually.
Beat well to remove lumps
Cook at once on a hot greased
griddle pan.

2 teaspoons of molasses may be
added before cooking.

One of Louise's handwritten family recipes from her book. The whereabouts of the original are unknown. Image courtesy of Evalina Settle.

Night Before Buckwheat Cakes

1 cake yeast (2¼ teaspoons active dry yeast)
4 cups lukewarm water, divided
1 tablespoon salt
1 tablespoon molasses
2 cups dark buckwheat flour
1 cup white flour
1 teaspoon soda
3 teaspoons baking powder

The night before you want to make the cakes, dissolve the yeast in 2 cups of water. Add salt, molasses, buckwheat, and white flours. Cover and set on the kitchen table overnight. In the morning, stir in remaining 2 cups of water, soda, and baking powder. Pour ¼ cup batter for each pancake on a buttered, hot griddle. Serve at once.

Pancakes

1 egg
1 cup milk
2 cups flour, well sifted
2 teaspoons baking powder
Pinch nutmeg
1 teaspoon sugar
1 teaspoon salt
1 teaspoon vanilla
Lard or butter for the griddle

In a small mixing bowl, beat egg and milk. Set aside. In a separate bowl, blend flour, baking powder, nutmeg, sugar, and salt. Add vanilla and stir until smooth. Place a small amount of lard (or butter) on a heated iron griddle. Pour about ¼ cup batter onto the griddle;

flip cake when it begins to bubble and edges turn slightly brown. When the bottom is lightly browned, remove from the pan.

Pancakes were served on the table with a set of small pitchers containing hot melted butter, hot maple syrup, and a small bowl of cinnamon sugar.

Baking Powder Biscuits

2 cups flour
2 teaspoons baking powder
½ teaspoon salt
Lard the size of an egg (4 tablespoons lard or butter)
Approximately ¾ cup milk

Preheat oven to 400°. Sift dry ingredients together. Cut lard into the flour mixture with two knives until the lard is in small pieces, the size of peas. Make a well in the middle of the flour and pour in just enough milk until the dough comes together. Stir milk into flour mixture until well blended. If it is too crumbly add more milk and if too sticky, add a bit more flour. Work up dough quickly, as overworking will make the biscuits too hard. Shape into a ball and place on a floured board. Pat or roll out to ½-inch thickness and cut with a biscuit cutter. Place on a cookie sheet and bake until lightly brown in the oven for about 10–12 minutes.

Oranges were a rarity during this time and considered a delicacy. In early winter, the trains would bring them up from the South when they were in season, and it was such a treat to have the fresh citrus fruit. The Cromwell children received an orange as a special gift in their Christmas stockings, a custom that Elizabeth continued when she had her own children. Elizabeth, long inclined to prevent food waste, continued the tradition of making the most of her fresh citrus just like Cuz taught her. As the fruit began to overripen, it would be made into marmalade to last through the remaining cold months.

Orange Marmalade

1 dozen oranges
5 lemons
8 quarts water
Granulated sugar

This recipe will take at least three days to prepare. On day one, slice citrus very thin, rind and all, and remove the seeds. Let stand for 24 hours in the water. On day two, heat the mixture to a boil, stirring constantly, and boil for 1 hour. Remove from heat and let sit for another 24 hours. On day three, measure 1 cup of sugar to each cup of orange mixture. Blend sugar into the fruit mixture and bring to a boil. Cook over low heat until sheeting stage.* Pour into sterilized jars and place the lids tight while the marmalade is still hot.

Country Sausage

8 pounds pork fat
12 pounds lean pork
3 tablespoons rubbed sage
1 small teacup salt (scant ⅔ cup)
1 tablespoon black pepper

---

* To test, after sugar has been added and returned to a full boil, let boil for 5 minutes. Then continue boiling until it begins to thicken. With a small spoon, take a small amount of the liquid, let it cool slightly, and slowly let it drain from the edge of the spoon in a cooking pot. When two large drops form along the spoon edges and then combine to form one large drop, this is the sheeting stage: 200–222° on a cooking thermometer.

2 tablespoons red pepper
Cases (described below)
Lard

Cut the meat into even-sized strips and small chunks, and weigh accurately. Spread meat out on a large area and cover with seasonings. Rub meat well with the seasonings and begin grinding meat. With hands, work ground seasoned meat thoroughly to evenly distribute the spices. Form into a mass. Stuff into cases, using either cleaned intestines of the hog or long narrow bags of thin canvas or muslin. When cases are filled, dip them in melted lard, and hang in a cool, dry, dark place.

John Cromwell called his sixth child by the nickname "Kid," although no one in the family knew why. They speculate that it was because of Elizabeth's playful ways and wondered if she was known

The Cromwell home in Cynthiana, where the children grew up and created a sense of place for Elizabeth. UKL, Elizabeth Cromwell Kremer Papers, 2016ms043.

in the neighborhood as "that Cromwell Kid." Elizabeth grew up in a house next door to the Christian church located on the corner of Main and Mill Streets. Her father was a member of the Christian church and her mother a member of the Presbyterian church located a block and a half away. The family had the freedom to take part in either of the church's services or activities. When no adults were around, the Cromwell children would sometimes go next door to the Christian church and climb into the baptismal font, the piece of furniture that held a basin of water, to play baptism. Their reenactments of weddings and funerals seemed to be a lasting happy moment in all their memories. After a morning of adventure, a classic midday meal from Louise's handwritten cookbook includes creamed oysters, corn fritters, and chan tart.

Creamed Oysters

1 tablespoon butter
1 tablespoon flour
1 pint thick cream
1 egg, well beaten
1 pint or more fresh oysters with liquor
Salt
Pepper

In a coffee cup, cream butter and flour with a fork until smooth. Set aside. Heat the bottom pan of a double boiler to a full boil. Pour cream into the top pan, stir in the egg, and blend well. Place the pan over the hot water. Stir in butter-flour mixture and blend well. Stir occasionally as the mixture begins to thicken. In a small saucepan, bring oysters to a boil in their own liquor; edges will curl. Do not overboil, as the oysters will become tough. Drain oysters and add to the double boiler mixture. Remove from heat; season with salt and fresh ground pepper. Serve immediately.

Corn Fritters

2 cups cornmeal
1¼ cups flour
2 eggs, beaten well
1 level teaspoon baking powder
Melted lard or oil

Stir the first four ingredients together until well blended. In a heavy iron skillet, melt lard or oil until there is enough to allow the batter to float slightly. Heat to hot but not boiling. Drop batter by the teaspoonful in the hot fat. Fry until golden brown. Remove from skillet with a spatula and let rest on paper towel covered plate.

Chan Tart

7 eggs, whites only
2 cups granulated sugar
1 tablespoon vinegar
1 teaspoon vanilla

Preheat oven to 300°. Beat egg whites until frothy and add other ingredients. Continue beating until the mixture is light and stands in peaks. Spread meringue in the bottom of two lightly buttered cake pans. Bake in the slow oven for about 40 minutes. Turn out gently onto a clean cloth and allow to dry.

For the filling

2 cups fresh-cut strawberries or sliced peaches
2 cups whipping cream

Wash, clean, and halve strawberries, or wash and slice peaches. Set aside. When ready to assemble the tart, whip the cream until stiff. Place one tart on a serving platter and spread with ⅓ of the whipped cream. Arrange strawberries or peaches on the surface, then coat the bottom of the other tart with another ⅓ of the whipped cream. Invert cream side on top of fruit. Spread the remaining cream on the top tart shell. Top with 3 strawberries that still have their green stems or a slice of peach. Serve immediately.

One day, Elizabeth confessed that she took a horse and buggy on one of her "Cromwell Kid's" escapades. She unhitched the animal and buggy from the front of the Presbyterian church while the adults were having a meeting. At the mature age of eight, she drove a few of her friends around the courthouse two blocks away from the church. She later said that she never forgot that incident because the harness was damaged during her heist. John and Eva made her take responsibility to pay for the repair by doing chores. Perhaps, this early adventure influenced Elizabeth's choice to never get a driver's license. Even though she did own a car, she preferred to have others drive.

The water supply for Cynthiana came from a huge, black water tower that the locals called the "stovepipe." Elizabeth described it as looming over the town from the top of the highest hill. It stood dark and tall, just waiting to topple on her as she passed beneath the giant on her way to visit her friends. She said, "I always drew in my breath and held it just in case it fell as I was passing. That way I had plenty of air in my lungs to survive the deluge of water."

Another favorite family memory that Elizabeth and her siblings never got tired of telling was the story of the silver balls. For an average family in the early 1900s, a fancy cake decorated with silver dragées was a luxury and the ultimate treat to top a special occasion cake. The tiny imported French metallic sugar spheres were not commonly found on the grocer's shelf. However, for the twenty-fifth wedding anniversary of Elizabeth's aunt and uncle, Lizzie Berry Jewell and Asa Jewell, the family went all out. The Cromwell family gathered with their closest cousins, the Dawsons and the Jewells, at Jewell's Corner in Jessamine County, Kentucky, for the special occasion. A huge meal was prepared, and the highlight of the event was a white cake covered with white icing decorated with silver dragées known to the children as silver balls.

When the cake was served, the silver balls were all gone! As the children were lined up and questioned, it was the consensus that the youngest and generally mischievous Cromwell daughter, Elizabeth, was the guilty party even though she protested the accusation. Twenty-five years later, when Aunt Lizzie and Uncle Asa celebrated their fiftieth wedding anniversary, their daughter, Frances Jewell McVey hosted another party for her mother and father. All the relatives who attended the first celebration were invited to join the party again. A telegram arrived from one of the Dawson "boys," who was then living in New York City, to relay his regrets. The telegram read, "I ate the silver balls! Love Jack."

White Cake

5 cups flour, sifted twice, divided
2 teaspoons baking powder
1 cup fresh butter
1 cup milk
12 egg whites
3 cups sugar
Sugar icing

Preheat oven to 350°. In one of the cups of flour, add the baking powder and blend well; set aside. In a large mixing bowl, cream butter until smooth and light. Alternately, stir in the other cups of flour and the milk, adding the flour–baking powder mixture last. In a separate bowl, beat egg whites until frothy. Gradually add sugar to eggs and whip until stiff. Fold the egg mixture in the flour mixture, blending well between additions. Line two 9-inch cake pans with buttered paper. Bake until lightly browned and sides begin to pull away from the cake pans. Let cool and dry before icing.

Sugar Icing

1 pound extra refined sugar or powdered sugar
1 ounce fine white cornstarch
¼ cup corn syrup
3 egg whites
1 teaspoon vanilla or rum flavoring

Add sugar to the corn syrup and cornstarch. Blend and set aside. Beat egg whites until frothy. Gradually add small amounts of sugar mixture, and beat constantly. Add desired flavoring and whip for 30 minutes with an eggbeater. Spread on bottom layer of the cooled cake. Top with remaining layer; ice top and sides. Decorate with silver dragées.

Another one of Elizabeth's childhood stories that left a lasting impression involved a monument at Cynthiana's Battle Grove Cemetery. The cemetery was established after the last raid of John Hunt Morgan during the Civil War. It is located on thirty-eight acres where the Civil War Battle of Cynthiana took place. Between the evergreen and magnolia trees are beautiful, sculpted statues; among them is the Withers Monument, commonly referred to as the "Little Boy Statue." The monument is a life-size young boy dressed in the fashion of his time, leaning lightly with his elbow on a stack of books. One of Elizabeth's siblings told her that the child that lay beneath the stone had died from eating green cherries. Neither Elizabeth nor either of her daughters ever ate a green cherry!

Holidays and memorials played a significant role in Elizabeth's life and in the memory of her daughters. Evalina and Pem went with their parents to Cynthiana to gather at Louise's house on Mill Street for Thanksgiving, Christmas, weddings, and funerals. Elizabeth's family gathered there, where Elizabeth's sister Louise organized and supplied food for both celebrations and bereaving families and friends of the recently departed.

Louise was regarded as the matriarch and superior cook of the Cromwell clan. She was considered the authority on all recipes, and if she did not know about something, it was not considered worth eating. She had a certain order in running her kitchen, and no relatives or visitors were going to upset that routine. All "outsiders" were banned from her kitchen as she single-handedly prepared and elegantly served many wonderful meals. Louise's handwritten recipes were kept in a small, leather-bound bank deposit book from the National Bank of Cynthiana. Her recipes include many of the favorite foods from the Cromwell family's daily meals, and most of the following recipes are from her handwritten cookbook.

Russian Dressing for Spring Leaf Lettuce

1 teaspoon salt
¼ cup apple cider vinegar
½ teaspoon paprika
1 teaspoon lemon juice

1 tablespoon green pepper, finely chopped
2 tablespoons chili sauce
½ cup olive oil

In a dressing bottle, place salt, vinegar, paprika, lemon juice, green pepper, and chili sauce. Close the bottle and shake vigorously until well blended. Add oil to the bottle and shake again. Store in the refrigerator until ready to serve. Arrange freshly washed and dried leaf lettuce in a shallow side bowl. Place fresh sliced tomatoes and top with thinly sliced sweet onion. Remove dressing from the refrigerator and let sit before serving.

Icebox Rolls

2–3 cups sifted flour
1 teaspoon baking powder
½ teaspoon soda
½ cake yeast (2¼ teaspoons active dry yeast)
1 pint milk
½ cup lard

Preheat oven to 350°. In a large bowl, blend dry ingredients together; make a well in the center and set aside. Dissolve yeast in a small amount of warm water. Place milk in a saucepan and scald. Skim off film and stir lard into milk until melted. When the milk pan is cool enough to touch the bottom of the pan, stir in the dissolved yeast. Slowly add liquid mixture into the flour well, stirring constantly. If necessary, work with your hands. When dough is well blended, form into a ball and place in a bowl. Cover with a damp, warm cloth and place it in the refrigerator for 2 hours or up to 3 days. When ready to bake, roll out dough and cut with a biscuit cutter. This dough can also be shaped as a cloverleaf, Parker House, or other shaped roll. Let rise and bake in the moderate oven for around 15–20 minutes or until the tops are golden brown.

Kentuckians have long enjoyed fresh game during hunting seasons, and it was a great time for a visit to Louise's Cynthiana dinner table. Her husband Earl would bring home game for all to enjoy, and quail was a particular favorite.

Broiled Quail

Quail
Butter
Salt and pepper
Strip of bacon per bird

Carefully cut out all the shot. Wash thoroughly but quickly, using a touch of soap in the water. Rinse several times and dry with a clean cloth. Split each bird down the back. Rub the bird with soft butter on both sides. Season with salt and pepper. Place on a gridiron with a strip of bacon under each bird. This will keep the skillet from getting too dry. The inside of the breast should be down. It may become necessary to add a little water if the drippings seem to be cooking away. Broil slowly on a low setting for 15–20 minutes. Turn several times during cooking. Bird will be done when a fork is inserted easily into the meat. Serve with a cream gravy.

Cream Gravy

1½ cups strained bacon fat
2 tablespoons flour
2 cups milk
Salt and pepper to taste

In a heavy skillet over medium heat, begin heating fat. Add flour and stir constantly with a spatula to keep from sticking. When flour starts to bubble, gradually stir in the milk. Do this slowly to control thickness. Bring to the boiling point and add seasoning to taste.

Stuffed Peppers

6–8 bell peppers
3 cups ground round
1 small onion, finely chopped
1 rounded teaspoon butter
1 egg
1 tablespoon cream
1 fresh tomato, skinned and chopped
Salt and pepper
1 cup bread crumbs

Preheat oven to 350°. Wash, cut the tops off the peppers, and seed. Brown meat and drain on a cloth. Sauté onion in butter. In a large bowl, beat egg with cream; then add onions, tomatoes, seasoning, bread crumbs, and meat. Gently toss with a fork until well blended. Fill pepper shells with meat mixture. Arrange in a shallow baking dish and bake in the moderate oven until peppers look and feel tender.

Combination Salad

1 envelope Knox gelatin
1 cup cold water
3 lemons, juiced and strained
1 cup sugar
1 fresh cucumber, thinly sliced
½ cup celery, finely chopped
1 cup fresh chopped pineapple

In a medium metal bowl, sprinkle gelatin on cold water and allow to soften. In a small saucepan, bring lemon juice and sugar to a boil over low heat, stirring constantly until sugar is dissolved. Then pour boiled juice over gelatin. Stir slowly and mix well. Let stand until gelatin cools slightly and begins to congeal. Place cucumbers, celery, and pineapple in individual molds. Slowly add gelatin and refrigerate until set. Remove from mold and serve on fresh lettuce. Place a small amount of mayonnaise on top of salad and top with mint leaves.

Country ham spread on beaten biscuits was a favorite with all the Cromwells and later enjoyed by the Kremer family. The little crisp biscuits kept fresh for months in tins. They were a treat at picnics, and when traveling, they made an excellent and filling meal. There is definitely an art to making beaten biscuits. Elizabeth's sister Louise especially liked the old recipe and loved to share its instructions with anyone who was interested. She felt that the biscuit's suggested cooking utensils were important items in a woman's kitchen.

"Modern" kitchen equipment later replaced the axe and mallet. A beaten biscuit or kneading table machine became available; it was a convenience for the job. The table had a marble slab with a mechanism of wringers, and a handle for turning was mounted at one end of the tabletop. When the dough was ready to be kneaded, it was fed into the wringers with one hand, and the other hand would turn the handle and work the dough through. Each time the dough was run through the wringers, the air bubbles would be forced out with a popping sound. As the dough neared readiness, the popping would be louder, and when the popping reached a loud bang, similar to a shotgun sound, the dough was ready.

Old Recipe Beaten Biscuits

2 pints flour
1 tablespoon lard
1 teaspoon salt
Milk

Mix into a stiff dough with equal parts milk and water. Beat for 30 minutes with an axe kept for the purpose.—Mrs. Martin. Recipe from *House Keeping in the Blue Grass*, Presbyterian Church, Missionary Society (Paris, Kentucky, 1879).

Beaten Biscuits

1 full teaspoon salt
2 rounded tablespoons lard
1 quart flour
Equal parts ice water and cold milk
1 level teaspoon baking powder (optional)

Preheat oven to 350°. Mix into a stiff dough. Work on a kneader, or beat with a mallet until smooth and glossy. If you use a kneader, run the dough back and forth until it is rather soft and perfectly smooth. Roll out and cut with a medium biscuit cutter. Pierce with a fork in the center. Bake in the moderate oven for 20–25 minutes. Let cool and dry. Place in tins for storage.

In their early childhood years, Evalina and Pem thought that Cynthiana was the hub of the universe. For their mother, it truly was. After Elizabeth graduated from college and began her career, she never went back to Cynthiana to live permanently, but she never left it completely behind. The town was her heritage, central to much of her work, and it remained for her a foundation of self-assurance.

2

The College Student

In 1917, John and Eva took their youngest children, Elizabeth and Jim, to National City, California. Elizabeth's father had health problems and went to California "for a rest." In April 1917, the United States officially entered World War I, so perhaps his health issues and the worldwide political situation were connected. Elizabeth's parents did not discuss personal matters, so it is unclear what prompted this move. Their oldest son, Henry, was employed in National City as a chemist at the Hercules Potash plant during World War I, and he advised John to come to California when his health "broke down." Henry assumed all financial responsibility for their trip, and John wrote after his death, "When I think now of those blessed eighteen months with him in California, I feel that all the gold in the world could not purchase it." For a time, sixteen-year-old Elizabeth was a West Coast resident who attended National City High School. During that time, she took advantage of the beach and developed a love of boating. Her passion for fresh fruits started in California and resulted in a desire to include fresh fruit dishes on every menu she created as she moved through her career.

Ambrosia ("Food for the gods")

3 oranges (peeled, seeded, and cut into wedges)
¼ cup flaked coconut
½ cup fresh pineapple (sliced and cut into chunks)
1 apple (unpeeled, thinly sliced, and cut into small pieces)
4 tablespoons sugar
2 bananas (peeled and cut into thin slices)
2 tablespoons fruit brandy

Gently toss together the first five ingredients until sugar is dissolved. Add banana slices (they are added last to prevent bruising). Chill well and serve in stemmed glass dessert cups.

Returning to Cynthiana, Elizabeth earned enough credits to complete high school a year early. "Miss Liz," her nickname at Cynthiana High School, graduated that spring. The following August, she applied and received certification to teach elementary school in the Commonwealth of Kentucky. She then accepted a position in rural Scott County. She said it was literally a one-room, little red schoolhouse. Laughing, she recalled that many of the students were heads taller than her and that some were even older than she was. Elizabeth hated teaching. But for five months, she taught, earning sixty-five dollars a month, which was all she needed to enroll at the University of Kentucky in January 1921 for her first semester.

By the fall semester of 1921, it was clear that Elizabeth was going to have to find a job to afford completing her college education. American companies were very involved in the production and marketing of sugar as well as with building roads and infrastructure in Cuba to facilitate increased sugar production to

Elizabeth on horseback (left) during one of her trips to Cuba. UKL,
Elizabeth Kremer Cromwell Papers, 2016ms043.

meet the demands of the US economy. Many jobs were available before World War I for young adults to begin careers. Elizabeth's sister, Belle, had gone to Cuba in 1916 to teach American workers' children on Cuban sugar plantations. By 1921, Belle had met and married Arthur Walsh and had two sons. In September 1921, Belle, her son John, and Elizabeth made the trip to Ensenada de Mora, Cuba.

Elizabeth had a contract to teach in Cuba for the fall and spring terms, but by February, her last three students were gone. The sugar industry was struggling, and the American families were being transferred out of Cuba. She stayed until May, as required by her contract, and she spent her free time exploring the country, riding horses, and enjoying the many local dishes and regional foods. She recalled that the meals were colorful and that everyday dining was an elegant event. Cuban cooking, she felt, strongly reflected its Spanish heritage in both cuisine and service.

Gazpacho

Always use fresh crisp vegetables.

> 4 large ripe tomatoes
> 1 large cucumber
> ½ small red onion
> 1 clove garlic (sliced)
> 3 tablespoons sherry
> ½ cup olive oil
> 2 cups tomato juice
> ½ teaspoon ground cumin
> ¼ or more hot pepper (chopped)

Peel and seed tomatoes and cucumber. Peel onion. Finely chop or grate all vegetables. Cut garlic in slices to release flavor. Combine all ingredients in an earthen or glass bowl, cover, and refrigerate.

Chill for 2 or 3 hours. Remove the garlic slices. Stir soup lightly and ladle into shallow soup bowls. Soup may be garnished with any of the following:

Cooked pieces of shrimp, crab meat, lobster, or ham
Slices of Spanish olives
Sliced or cubed avocado
Minced parsley
Seasoned bread crumbs

Baked Fish

2 pounds fish filets
2 lemon wedges
Salt and pepper
Fresh parsley, chopped

Preheat oven to 350°, possibly raising to 375° during the cooking process. Place fish in a buttered baking dish. Season with salt and pepper, and sprinkle with parsley. Squeeze lemon over fish pieces. Bake for 30 minutes, basting often. Fish is done when it flakes easily with a fork. Serve immediately.

Arroz con Pollo

6 skinless chicken breasts
Olive oil
1 can (6 ounces) tomato paste
1 clove garlic
1 medium onion, chopped
½ teaspoon salt
¼ teaspoon ground black pepper
1½ cups water
½ cup uncooked rice

For chicken garnish, have cooked and kept warm to assemble:

> Pimiento strips
> Asparagus, cooked
> 1 can tiny early peas
> 4 slices green pepper, chopped

In a dutch oven, brown chicken breasts in ¼ inch of olive oil until tender and golden brown. Drain off oil. Remove the chicken and set aside, covering to keep warm. Place the tomato paste, garlic, onion, salt, pepper, and water in the dutch oven, and stir lightly until well blended. Heat to boiling and add rice. Cook over low heat until rice is done, add additional water if necessary. Place cooked rice on a large serving dish. Place chicken pieces on rice and surround them with peas, peppers, and asparagus decoratively. Top with pimiento strips.

Fruit Salad

> Avocado
> Grapefruit
> Leaf lettuce
> Mint
> Fruit salad dressing

Peel and slice avocado and grapefruit; use about 3 slices of each for each individual salad. Place 2 lettuce leaves on a salad plate; arrange avocado and grapefruit alternately in a pinwheel pattern. Place a sprig of mint in the center. Drizzle a small amount of dressing over salad before serving.

Fruit Salad Dressing

> ¼ teaspoon salt
> ⅛ teaspoon ground pepper

¼ teaspoon paprika
1 sliced garlic clove
½ cup red or white wine vinegar
1 tablespoon lemon juice
¼ cup olive oil

Stir salt, pepper, paprika, and garlic into vinegar. Whisk lemon and oil into seasoning.

Lime Drink

1 cup granulated sugar
2 cups warm water
1 lime (cut into 6 wedges)

Dissolve sugar in warm water. Cut lime and place sugar water and 2 lime wedges in a glass container with a tight lid. Let stand until ready to use. In a 12-ounce drinking glass, firmly squeeze the juice out of 2 lime wedges; drop the wedges into the bottom of the glass. Add ½ cup of the sugar water and ⅔ cup drinking water; fill the glass with ice.

If the limes are small, use more wedges. For a little sweeter drink, add more sugar water and less drinking water. Be sure to remove old lime skins before fixing a refill, to keep the drink from becoming bitter.

Returning to the University of Kentucky in September 1921 as a second-term freshman, Elizabeth made up her missed semesters by later taking summer school. She moved into Patterson Hall, the women's dormitory, on the UK campus. Her room fee was one dollar a day, and this included meals served on the second floor of the dormitory.

The dining room in the University of Kentucky Patterson Hall dormitory, around 1910. UKL, Glass Plate Negative Collection, 2007ua014.

Junket was often served at "Pat Hall," according to Betsy Helburn Strisower, Elizabeth's friend and classmate. Junket was meant to be prepared in a small, stemmed dessert cup, but at Patterson Hall, it was made in an oblong glass dish to serve a larger crowd. The first person to insert their spoon got the dessert the way it was meant to be presented—in a custard stage—but once the spoon broke, the surface of the junket dissolved into a liquid state. Betsy said it was truly awful and claimed that the mental picture lingered more than seventy years later. Those who were interviewed did not have many positive memories of the food in Patterson Hall, other than the fact that the meals included a lot of starches and fried dishes. However, they did have fond memories of some of the popular sweets, like candy pudding, and that candy making was a big part of their college socializing. Many of the following were recipes the students cooked together on Saturday evening or Sunday afternoon in the dormitory kitchen.

Junket, or Vanilla Rennet Custard

1 cup milk
4 teaspoons granulated sugar
½ teaspoon vanilla
1 tablet rennet
2 teaspoons cold water

Have ready dessert cups to be filled with custard. In a small saucepan, combine milk, sugar, and vanilla. Stir until sugar is dissolved.

In a separate small cup, place crushed rennet tablet and water. Stir to dissolve the tablet. Heat milk mixture to lukewarm (baby bottle temperature). Add the table mixture to the saucepan ingredients. Stir to blend. Pour into dessert cups. Let stand at room temperature. When set, place in the refrigerator. Serve and eat immediately. Makes 2 servings. Recipe and instructions given by Betsy Helburn Strisower.

Notes on Candy Making from the 1920s

It is important to remember in making candy that it must be cooked to the proper stage. After inserting the thermometer into the boiling candy, watch it carefully, but never lift it from the mixture.

Cover the pan for the first 3 minutes of boiling. It will produce steam that will prevent too many crystals from forming on the sides of the pan. Wipe away any crystals from the sides with a damp cloth towel.

Weather conditions are important when making candy. It is impossible to make hard candies in a hot, moist atmosphere.

Use a heavy saucepan large enough to allow the mixture to boil without running over (four times larger than the total ingredients).

Marble slabs are ideal. However, buttered or oiled enamel tabletops may be used.

In making pull candy, gloves may be used. Grease them lightly and dust with flour or cornstarch. If bare hands are preferred, have a large bowl of ice water and continually dip your hand when necessary.

When a candy recipe calls for cream, heat it quickly, as slow cooking may make it curdle.

Candy Pudding

6 cups granulated sugar
3 cups heavy cream
Grated fresh coconut, chopped nuts, and candied fruit to suit your taste

Place sugar and cream in a large saucepan and stir well. Cook over low heat until the mixture forms a hard ball in cold water, generally, when the syrup forms thick, rope-like threads when you lift it with a spoon. Alternatively, the temperature should read 250–260° on a candy thermometer. Pour out onto a marble slab. When it cools, work with a wooden spoon until it creams. Add fresh coconut, nuts, and candied fruit. Put in a mold or use waxed paper to roll into a tube. Place in the refrigerator for several hours. Slice in pieces of a desired size to serve.

Sea Foam

3 cups brown sugar
¼ teaspoon salt
1 cup water

2 egg whites, stiffly beaten
1 teaspoon vanilla
½ cup broken nutmeats

In a large saucepan, boil, without stirring, sugar, salt, and water. Boil until a thread forms when a small amount is poured from a teaspoon. Pour this mixture very slowly into the beaten egg whites. Beat continuously until candy thickens. Stir in vanilla and nutmeats. Pour into a lightly buttered square pan and mark into squares.

Divinity

1 cup brown sugar
1 cup white sugar
⅓ cup light corn syrup
¼ teaspoon salt
½ cup cold water
2 egg whites, beaten
½ teaspoon vanilla
1 cup nuts

Put brown sugar, white sugar, corn syrup, salt, and water in a saucepan and cook. Stir until sugar is completely dissolved. Continue cooking without stirring until the hard, brittle stage; a candy thermometer will read 267° (if a thermometer is unavailable, drop a small amount of the mixture into ice water, and it will form a hard ball). Remove syrup from the fire and gradually pour in a fine stream over the beaten egg whites: beating all the while. After the addition, continue beating until the divinity will hold its shape when a small daub is dropped from a spoon. Add vanilla and broken nutmeats. Mix thoroughly and drop by teaspoon on waxed paper or pour in a slightly buttered pan and cut in squares when set.

Creamy Chocolate Fudge

3 cups granulated sugar
3 squares unsweetened chocolate
⅛ teaspoon salt
3 tablespoons light corn syrup
1 cup milk
3 tablespoons butter
1½ teaspoons vanilla extract
¾ cup nuts, chopped (optional)

Combine sugar, chocolate, salt, corn syrup, and milk in a deep saucepan that has a firm-fitting cover. Place uncovered pan over low heat. Blend without boiling until sugar is dissolved. Cover pan, cook over medium heat, and bring fudge to boiling. Stir occasionally to prevent the fudge from sticking to the pan bottom. Boil gently for 3–4 minutes. Uncover pan, place candy thermometer into fudge, and continue cooking until 236° (soft ball stage). When candy is at the right temperature, remove the pan from the burner and add butter and vanilla—do not stir. Cool to lukewarm. Beat briskly until fudge begins to stiffen and loses its shiny appearance. Stir in nuts and pour into a well-buttered square glass pan. Score top of fudge as it hardens. Let cool before cutting.

Pecan Pralines

3 tablespoons whitecorn syrup
2 cups granulated sugar
1 cup light brown sugar
1 large pinch of salt
1 cup evaporated milk
3 or 4 cups whole pecans
Butter the size of a large egg (4 tablespoons)
1 teaspoon vanilla

Blend corn syrup, sugars, salt, and milk in a large saucepan. Cook over low heat until the candy mixture forms a soft ball in iced water. Add nuts and cook again until candy forms a soft ball in iced water. Remove from fire and add butter and vanilla. Beat until creamy. Drop by teaspoonfuls onto waxed paper. Candy mixture should be runny enough to form a wafer under nuts.

Modjeskas

2 cups granulated sugar
2 cups heavy cream, heated; divided
1¼ cup light corn syrup
2 tablespoons butter
1 teaspoon vanilla extract
Marshmallows

Combine sugar, ½ cup of measured cream, and corn syrup in a 3- to 4-quart saucepan. Place over low heat. Stir gently until sugar is dissolved. Cover the pan and allow crystals to form and be washed down the pan sides in the condensing steam. While the sugar mixture is cooking, place remaining cream in a small saucepan to heat. Once the sugar mixture is ready, increase the heat to medium under the candy mixture. Keeping mixture at a constant boil, insert candy thermometer. Continue cooking over low heat until it reaches 238°–240°; remove from heat. Stir in butter and vanilla. Allow to cool for 10–15 minutes before dipping marshmallows. Drop individual marshmallows in caramel and remove quickly. Place them on candy paper. Twist paper ends when set. Store in a cool place. Recipe credited to Betsy Helburn Strisower.

These candies were created in the 1880s by Anton Busath, a French immigrant and Louisville, Kentucky, candymaker who had a shop on 445 West Fourth Street, near the Macauley Theater on 319 West Walnut Street (now Muhammad Ali Boulevard). He made the candies for some time but wanted to show his admiration for the Polish-born actress, Helena Modjeska, who often performed in downtown Louisville, by naming them after her. The candy became a highly desired sweet, and it was considered a great achievement to make.

Peanut Brittle

2 cups sugar
1 cup corn syrup
1 cup water
2 teaspoons butter
2 cups unsalted raw peanuts
1 teaspoon soda
1 teaspoon vanilla

Combine sugar, syrup, and water and stir until sugar is dissolved. Place over heat and bring to a boil, stirring occasionally. Insert candy thermometer and continue to cook until mixture has reached soft ball stage (230°–240°). Stir in butter and peanuts. Continue cooking until syrup is light brown and has reached a hard crack stage (280°). Remove from fire. Add soda and vanilla and blend well. Mix well and pour on a buttered marble slab or enamel tabletop, spreading as thin as possible with a wooden spoon. When almost cooled, dip hands in ice water and turn quickly, thinning more if desired. Break into pieces and store in tins.

Cream Pulled Candy

3 cups granulated sugar
1 tablespoon vinegar

½ cup cream
2 cups water
1 teaspoon vanilla

In a large saucepan, add sugar to vinegar and stir well. Add cream and mix well. Stir in water and blend until all sugar is dissolved. Cook until the candy mixture spins a thread when dropped from a teaspoon (260°). This may have to be increased to 5° more if the weather conditions are damp. Pour on a large marble slab or on a platter that has been rinsed with iced water. Add vanilla, mixing lightly with a fork. Cool and begin to pull until mixture is creamy and loses its gloss. Pull into a long strip and lay on a slab. Cut with scissors to desired size. When candy has dried, keep in a tin box to keep creamy.

Saratoga Chips were popular in the 1920s. A chef in Saratoga Springs, New York, began making this finger food. It was a great treat to be served at outdoor sporting events. Girls gathered in the dormitory kitchens and prepared these for their outings on the weekends.

Potato Chips

Medium-size baking potatoes
Lard
Salt

Use a deep enough pan to allow for bubbling and baking potato slices. Wash and peel potatoes. Cut in very thin slices and keep in ice water until ready to fry, as they will begin to turn dark in color if not kept moist and cold. Heat lard to hot. Temperature is right when a small cube of bread dropped into fat will become golden brown in 40 seconds. Work potatoes in small batches. Dry each potato slice on linen towels before placing in hot lard (water will cause the lard to splatter). Use a slotted spoon or skimmer and place potato slices in fat. Stir slowly and gently with a long-handled wooden spoon. When chips are a light brown, remove from fat with a skimmer. Place on towels to drain, and sprinkle immediately with salt. Place in brown paper bags.

Despite the questionable food at Patterson Hall, Elizabeth enjoyed her college time and discovered a love of theater performances in the UK, particularly the production of *Liliom*. She increased her love of poetry, expanding her repertoire from the Victorian traditions of Longfellow, Browning, and Tennyson to works of women poets like Eunice Tietjens, Adelaide Crapsey, and Edna St. Vincent Millay.

Elizabeth's aunts, Lizzie Berry Jewell and Norma Berry (wife of John D. Berry, Evalina Berry Cromwell's brother), opened the Pleasant View Inn on May 14, 1925. They served dinner (lunch) at 1:00 p.m., afternoon tea, and supper from 6:30 p.m.–7:30 p.m. The Pleasant View Inn, commonly referred to as Mrs. Jewell's Tea Room, was in Lizzie and husband Asa's country home at Jewell's Corner, on the road halfway from Lexington to Harrodsburg in Jessamine County (the site where I had my first conversation with Evalina Kremer Settle). Lizzie hired a few local girls along with Elizabeth to help prepare meals and serve the customers. She often used the Cromwell children during their summer college break to help with the business, and they liked earning money to assist with their college expenses. In fact, Elizabeth spent the summer of 1925 working at the Tea Room. As Elizabeth was finishing her college

The Jewell family's country home, Pleasant View, in Jessamine County, Kentucky. The home was referred to as Jewell's Corner, and it became the location of Jewell's Tea Room. UKL, Frances Jewell McVey Papers, 0000ua003.

degree at the University of Kentucky, Lizzie Jewell's Tea Room was becoming a success and was quite popular with Lexingtonians. Those who worked for Lizzie Jewell said she would work side by side with them in the hot kitchen. She wanted customers to be pleased with the food and the service and made sure of that herself. When the Tea Room first opened, they were closed on Sundays, but on July 25, 1926, they began a Sunday night supper under the management of Lizzie Jewell and Elizabeth Cromwell.

When everything was ready for service, Lizzie would go upstairs and dress for the occasion in her best clothes so that guests would think that she had not lifted a finger in preparing the meal. She was the "perfect hostess." Kathryn "Katy" McMurtry Staton, another one of Elizabeth's friends from childhood as well as college, remembered specifically the corn soup at the Tea Room. She would drive to Jewell's Corner from the university and have a delicious meal that sometimes started with this soup served in a Haviland soup dish with fresh popped corn floating on top.

Corn Soup

1 large potato, peeled and cut into cubes
1 small onion, cut into small pieces
2 cups fresh corn, cut from the cob*
5 cups milk
2 teaspoons butter
1 teaspoon granulated sugar
2 teaspoons salt
¼ teaspoon black pepper

Boil potatoes and onion in enough water to cover; cook until tender. Add corn and cook for 5–10 minutes. Drain off the water. Heat milk in the top of a double boiler. Rub corn and potato mixture through a food mill and stir in heated milk. When hot, add butter, sugar, salt, and pepper. Do not overcook, as soup will curdle, depending on the richness of the milk. Top with a few kernels of freshly popped corn.

In January 1924, Elizabeth pledged to the Kappa Kappa Gamma sorority and moved into the sorority house on Maxwell Street. She worked on the weekends and summers at the Tea Room to finance her activities and the completion of her degree. She had many stories about campus and social events, such as A. B. Happy Chandler serenading his dates while rowing a boat on the lake on the university's campus and trips out to the country to have

* Frozen corn may also be used.

The University of Kentucky's Kappa Kappa Gamma sorority house on 179 East Maxwell Street, 1931. UKL, Lafayette Studios Photographs, 96pa101.

picnics at the reservoir. The university president's home, Maxwell Place, was the location of many teas given by Frances Jewell McVey, wife of university president Frank McVey. Frances was the daughter of Lizzie and Asa Jewell. As Lizzie and Eva were sisters, the Cromwell family was welcome at Maxwell Place and sometimes put to work at social gatherings. Lizzie's menu choices for the Tea Room endured, as Frances used them frequently at Maxwell Place, and Elizabeth used variations of those recipes later in her own restaurant menus.

Brewing of Tea

Choose the flavor of tea desired. Tea should be made in a china or earthen pot. The tea flavor is sometimes spoiled if brewed in a metal pot. Allow one teaspoon of tea for every cup of boiling water. Be sure to heat the pot by rinsing with scalding water before brewing tea. Heat fresh cold water to a bubbling boil on the stove. Place tea in a hot pot and add a small amount of boiling water to the tea in the pot. Allow to steep 1 minute, and then pour in the rest of the hot water. Let this stand in a warm place for 2 minutes before serving. Using a tea sieve, pour the tea slowly and gently to keep tea leaves in the bottom of the pot.

Spiced Tea

2 sticks cinnamon
10 whole cloves
Grated rind of 1 lemon and 1 orange
2 tablespoons black tea
3 quarts water
Juice of 4 lemons, strained
Juice of 6 oranges, strained
2 cups sugar

Place spices and grated rind in a cheesecloth bag and tie. Place tea in a separate cheesecloth bag and tie, leaving room in the bag for the tea leaves to swell. Put cold water in a deep pot. Place tea and spice bags in the water and place over high heat. Cover and bring to a rolling boil. Remove from heat and steep for 5 minutes. Stir in juices. Add sugar and mix until dissolved. Remove cheesecloth bags. Keep hot until ready to serve. This recipe will serve 25 guests.

We Three Ice

3 lemons

3 oranges

3 bananas

3 cups sugar

3 pints water

1 pint cream

Peel all fruit and remove the seeds. Slice one lemon and one orange, and mix with sugar and water. In a saucepan, boil until sugar is dissolved. Cook; then add the juice from the rest of the lemons and oranges. Mash bananas and add to the fruit mixture. Blend well. Freeze in a metal ice tray or a loaf pan until mushy. Remove from the container and add cream, blending well. Return to the freezer for at least 4 hours. Serve in small dessert cups on saucers lined with paper doilies. This ice may be used as a base for fruit punch. Place ice in a punch bowl and add a bottle of ginger ale per recipe.

Cucumber Sandwich

1 large fresh cucumber

3 slices sweet onion (6 spring onions when in season)

2 tablespoons salt

2 cups water

Peel and slice cucumber and onion. Dissolve salt in the water and soak cucumber and onion slices in this mixture for 1 hour. Drain and grind in a meat grinder. Spread mayonnaise on bread and then spread on cucumber-onion mixture. Cut in 3-inch rectangular strips or diamond crosscut pieces and arrange on a china platter. Cover with a damp towel.

In preparing tea sandwiches, use very thinly sliced bread. The crust should be trimmed from the bread before adding sandwich spreads. It is best to have ready a large linen tea towel that you have rinsed in cool water and rung out tightly to a damp dry. As you place finished sandwiches on the platter, cover with the damp towel to keep the sandwiches from drying out. Sandwiches may be made ahead and be stored for a short time in the refrigerator with the towel as a cover.

Fried Chicken and Mush

Cut a young chicken in quarters. Allow one quarter per guest. Wash and wipe dry with a cloth towel. Season generously with salt and pepper. Cover with flour, being sure to dust under the wings and all parts of the leg and thigh quarter. Fry in a heavy iron skillet with enough melted lard (heated over medium-high) to measure 1 inch on the side of the skillet. Brown chicken on both sides. Reduce fire and cook until tender, turning often.[†] When finished, drain on a cloth towel before serving. Save seasoned flour for making gravy.

The home economics degree required Elizabeth to take a class in which she had to kill, pluck, and then prepare a chicken for cooking. She said that it was the most difficult course she took at the university; and she convinced a male colleague into killing the bird for her, and she took over from there.

[†] Take out 2–4 tablespoons of chicken grease to make gravy. Fry the mush in the chicken skillet, but make gravy in a clean one.

Country Gravy

2–4 tablespoons chicken grease
2–4 tablespoons seasoned flour
2 cups whole milk

Heat the chicken grease over medium heat and add an equal amount of seasoned flour. Stir in the flour and cook, stirring constantly for 2–3 minutes or until it is a very light golden color. Reduce the heat to low and whisk in milk very slowly. Continue stirring until the gravy is thickened. If it is too thick, add more milk one tablespoon at a time until you like the consistency. Remove from heat and add salt and pepper if necessary.

Mush

4–6 cups boiling water
1 cup watered ground cornmeal
1 teaspoon salt

Place boiling water in the top half of a double boiler and put on direct heat. With a wooden spoon, stir in cornmeal and salt to rapidly boiling water. Cook until thick, stirring constantly. Have the bottom pan ready with boiling water also, and put the top pan on the boiling water. Cook for 30 minutes. When cooked, remove from heat and pack mush firmly into greased loaf pans. Cover to prevent a crust from forming on top. Place in the refrigerator to set. Chill until firm. Slice in ½-inch thick pieces and dip in flour on both sides. Fry in the leftover chicken grease or melted butter. Fry to a golden brown on each side. When serving, place a chicken quarter beside the fried mush and top with country gravy.

Ginger Bread and Brown Sugar Sauce

2½ cups flour
½ cup sugar
½ teaspoon salt
1 teaspoon ginger
1 teaspoon cinnamon
½ teaspoon cloves
1½ teaspoons baking soda
½ cup butter
1 egg, well beaten
1 cup sorghum
1 cup buttermilk

Preheat oven to 325°. Sift flour, sugar, salt, ginger, cinnamon, cloves, and baking soda together. Cream butter and stir in beaten egg, sorghum, and buttermilk in a mixing bowl. Add flour mixture slowly by hand to egg mixture. When moistened, stir until well blended. Pour into a square greased baking pan. Bake for 1 hour.

Brown Sugar Sauce

¼ cup flour
1 cup brown sugar
1 cup boiling water
¼ cup butter
½ teaspoon vanilla

Mix flour and brown sugar well in a saucepan. Add boiling water. Cook sauce until it thickens. Remove from heat and add butter and vanilla. Mix well.

This is best served cut in squares and placed in individual, narrow-rimmed bowls. The hot sauce may be passed around in a small pitcher. Placing hot sauce in a small pitcher that has been set on a small saucer is always best, as the sauce will stay hotter.

On June 1, 1925, Elizabeth graduated from the University of Kentucky with a bachelor of science degree in home economics. She was Mortar Board president, YWCA cabinet secretary, member of the Pan Hellenic Council, Phi Upsilon Omicron, vice president of the Women's Administrative Council, vice president of the Agriculture Society, vice president of the Home Economics Club, and a member of the Women's Athletic Association.

Home economics graduates, 1925. Elizabeth Cromwell second from right (kneeling) and Betsy Helburn standing tallest in back. UKL, Elizabeth Kremer Cromwell Papers, 2016ms043.

Wrapped around her diploma, Elizabeth kept this charge from University of Kentucky president Frank McVey for the graduating class of 1925:

> On this commencement day you stand in a new relation to the University, to the State, and to Life. The University that has given you of its store of learning now looks upon you as its children. The State that regarded you as wards, now conceives of you as citizens, better equipped than the average to do your part. The battle of life, whose noise you have heard from time to time through the college gates, now calls for your participation as recruits in the struggle.
>
> If what you have learned while here has given you larger intellectual interests, and widened your powers of comprehension, the University feels a part of its duty done, and if in the doing character has become your possession and a part of your moral fiber, the State is satisfied with its investment of men and money.
>
> The university trusts you have learned to approach problems with open minds, to set aside prejudice in your judgment of men and affairs. It hopes that you may live in peace and happiness, though ready to fight for the right, at all times using your strength for the betterment of the community.
>
> May you have in your declining years, material comfort, the respect of your fellow citizens, the feeling of work well done, and a spiritual and intellectual interest in human life.
>
> Meantime, the University's honor is your honor. In your acts and deeds you now reflect your heritage.

To fellow man, the University is measured by your character, by your deeds, by the company you keep. It is in this spirit that I call upon you to be true to the larger things of life, to be men and women of courage, integrity, sympathy, and gentleness.

3

The Professional

In 1925, the summer immediately after receiving her degree, Elizabeth was contacted by the University of Kentucky for a job opportunity. The manager, Grace Bryan Hollister, of Lexington's Phoenix Hotel cafeteria was leaving her position to run the dining room at a Detroit, Michigan, women's club. By the 1920s, there were a number of women's clubs in major cities, and larger clubs had clubhouses with facilities for meetings, events, and classes for members. Men's and women's clubs were considered a big part of a young professional's life.

While the manager's position was being offered to the existing hostess, the hotel was interested in having Elizabeth and another woman from a Michigan college manage the kitchen. This was her first job out of college and her first experience with a French-trained chef. In a direct quote from Elizabeth, "A lot more was expected of us that we did not know how to do. We lasted three weeks and were fired." After being fired from her very first job in restaurant management, Elizabeth returned to Cynthiana to restore her self-esteem. She accomplished this and stayed connected by entertaining her friends and utilizing her kitchen skills.

Her friend Katy remembered that during that time, Elizabeth hosted a birthday tea party for her at the Cromwell home. Around 1926, Katy was in Cynthiana for a short visit with her new baby. Elizabeth made an angel food cake and fresh-squeezed lemonade. Katy remembered the angel food cake as perfect, without any glaze or frosting.

Angel Food Cake from Scratch

Eggs should be as fresh as possible; whites should be cold when separated from the yolks but at room temperature when beaten. Do not grease the cake container, a tube pan, and make sure all utensils are free from all oil and grease. For easy removal, a piece of waxed paper may be cut to fit the bottom of the tube pan. Use a very thin knife to run around the sides of the baked cake to loosen it from the sides of the pan.

1 cup cake flour
1½ cups confectioners' sugar, sifted
1½ cups egg whites
½ teaspoon salt
1 teaspoon vanilla
1½ teaspoons cream of tartar
1 cup granulated sugar

Preheat oven to 325°. Sift together flour and confectioners' sugar three times. With a wire whisk beat egg whites until frothy. Add salt, cream of tartar, and vanilla; beat until stiff and glossy but not dry. Add granulated sugar one tablespoon at a time. Using a motion of down-up-over, fold and blend well.

Gently distribute the cake batter evenly in an ungreased tube pan. Bake for 50–60 minutes or until golden brown. Before removing the cake, place it over a bottle or large funnel on a counter. This will allow currents of air to pass under and over as the cake cools and dries. Cake may be iced, sprinkled with powdered sugar, or served with a sugared fruit and topped with unsweetened cream. Garnish with a sprig of mint leaves.

A determined woman, Elizabeth continued to be interested in restaurant work despite her questionable start. She thought she would broaden her opportunities, and so, not lingering long in Cynthiana, Elizabeth took advantage of her connection with Grace Hollister. In August 1926, she left Cynthiana for Detroit to be Grace's assistant manager of the Detroit City Club, managed by the Women's City Club. Through the club's first three decades, it grew to be one of the largest women's clubs in the world and hosted many chapters of women's clubs, including the League of Women Voters. After a brief stint in Detroit, Elizabeth moved closer to home to work in the dietetic department of Childs Restaurant in Cincinnati but, in 1927, was sent to a job at a Childs

Childs logo, from a menu in Elizabeth Kremer's personal papers, 2016ms043.

in New York City, likely due to the closing of the Cincinnati restaurant. Childs restaurants were in many major cities. They were known for their stand-up counters, small tables for two, and white tiles on the floors and walls. Childs specialized in quick, good, cooked meals. The restaurants were clean and efficiently run to please the customer. You could have excellent breakfast, lunch, or dinner and all you could eat at any time. The restaurant served many egg dishes, breakfast breads, and creamed chipped beef on toast. There were a number of locations around New York City. The talk was that there were great opportunities in the restaurant field in the heart of the big city.

Creamed Chipped Beef on Toast

2 tablespoons butter
12 ounces dried beef, finely chopped
2–3 tablespoons flour
1½ cups milk
Salt and pepper to taste
Piece of toasted bread with crust removed

In a heavy skillet, melt butter over low fire. Stir in chopped beef. Sprinkle in flour, stirring constantly with a spatula to prevent sticking and scorching. Heat until flour is bubbly but not browned. Gradually add milk and salt and pepper to taste, remove from fire, and serve on a piece of crisp toast with crust removed.

Elizabeth D. Reynolds, a member of the Cynthiana Lebus family, operated a restaurant in New York City at Fifteenth and Forty-Eighth Streets. Known as Schrafft's Restaurant, it had become a very popular and successful eating establishment. This gave Elizabeth Cromwell a Kentucky connection in New York, and she worked for Reynolds for a brief time. Elizabeth learned that she could receive training, hands-on experience, and excellent management skills at Schrafft's. The owner of the restaurant chain was Frank G. Shattuck, who was a salesperson for the Schrafft Company in upstate New York. Schrafft's started as a candy store, and Shattuck's sister, Jane, was largely responsible for the introduction of light lunches into the stores. The Schrafft's restaurants served complete meals in dining rooms and sold bakery goods and candies. By the late 1920s, there were many Schrafft's located in New York City.

Elizabeth, who was terrible with names, did recall Gerald Shattuck, the youngest of Frank's sons, who was in charge of her training. She said it was like army training: everyone was expected to start at the bottom and work every position. That way, all parts of the restaurant operations became common knowledge, and everyone was cross-trained. One position Elizabeth related to her friend Katy was her time as "salad girl": "Never forget, Katy, when you order coleslaw at a restaurant, some poor girl is back in the hot kitchen laboriously chopping heads of cabbage." Elizabeth believed that hand-cut vegetables were always best and that, even though there were many kitchen devices designed to save time, the vegetables got bruised in the whirling blades.

Coleslaw

1 medium cabbage
½ medium onion
Salt and pepper
Boiled dressing
Paprika

Shred one medium cabbage; soak in iced water until crisp. Drain and dry between cloth towels. Chop onion finely and toss with shredded cabbage in a large bowl. Season with salt and pepper to taste. Add enough boiled dressing to moisten well. Blend in dressing. Taste and add more dressing or seasoning, as cabbage will differ in strength according to freshness. Serve in a bowl lined with large lettuce leaves. Sprinkle with paprika, and garnish with a large sprig of parsley.

Boiled Dressing

2 tablespoons flour
1 teaspoon dry mustard
⅔ tablespoon sugar
⅛ teaspoon cayenne pepper
¼ tablespoon salt
1 or 2 egg yolks, slightly beaten
2 tablespoons butter
¾ cup milk or ½ cup water
¼ cup apple cider vinegar

Separate eggs and set aside. Sift dry ingredients. On top of a double boiler, combine dry ingredients, egg yolks, butter, and milk or water. Stir the vinegar in slowly. Stir and cook over boiling water until the mixture begins to thicken. Strain and cool.

At Elizabeth Reynolds's restaurant, the lunch menu included Kentucky fried chicken with cream gravy, green beans, and zucchini squash; the price was ninety-five cents. Another lunch option was fresh salmon loaf with egg sauce, a recipe that was considered a "Cynthiana hometown dish." The salmon loaf and

"KENTUCKY SERVES A MEAL"

Elizabeth D. Reynolds menu, from Elizabeth Kremer's
personal papers, 2016ms043.

egg sauce recipes came from the handwritten family recipe book
kept by Elizabeth's oldest sister Louise.

Fresh Salmon Loaf with Egg Sauce*

2 cups fresh cooked salmon
1 egg, unbeaten
1½ cups bread crumbs
½ cup milk
2 teaspoons lemon juice
¼ teaspoon salt
¼ teaspoon pepper

---

* This was served with parsley potatoes and fresh asparagus.

Preheat oven to 350°. Poach fresh salmon until flaky. Remove all bones and skin. Grind in a meat grinder. Add egg to ground fish and blend gently with a fork. Alternatively stir in bread crumbs, milk, lemon juice, and seasoning. Mix well. Pack fish mixture into a small, well-greased loaf pan that has the bottom lined with waxed paper.

Bake in the medium oven until lightly browned. Remove and let stand for 5 minutes. Turn out onto a platter.

Egg Sauce

3 eggs
¼ stick butter

Boil eggs to a hard boil. Remove shells and chop eggs. Place butter in a small saucepan and melt over low heat. Add eggs and stir gently until eggs are covered with butter but not sizzling in fat. Pour over the loaf, and garnish with fresh parsley sprigs before serving. If serving individual plates, slice loaf 1 inch thick, top with egg butter sauce, garnish with fresh parsley sprigs, and serve immediately.

While working on becoming one of the only women managers, Elizabeth recalled a confrontation she had with a disagreeable cleaning man. She remembered that her eyes filled with tears because, when she told Shattuck about the incident, his only reply was "Can you take this work or not?" With an answer of "I took it!" she decided that from then on, she would always be able "to take it."

In the early 1920s, most of Schrafft's restaurants were located in the business districts of the city, but Frank Shattuck

Schrafft's menu, from Elizabeth Kremer's personal papers, 2016ms043.

decided to expand to more residential areas. A new Schrafft's restaurant opened at Seventy-Third and Broadway. It was named "Upper Broadway," and Elizabeth Cromwell was its new manager. Schrafft's menus included the following suggestions for their Club Dinner ($1.35).

Cape Cod Clam Chowder

2 slices pork jowl, diced
1 onion, sliced
1 cup water
3 large potatoes, peeled and diced
1 teaspoon salt
Pepper to taste
1½ dozen clams, chopped fine (save the liquor)
1 quart milk
Crackers, crumbled
Parsley, finely chopped
2 tablespoons butter and 2 tablespoons flour for thickening (optional)

In an iron skillet, fry the pork. Do not overcook. Add onion and fry slightly. In a large soup pot, place together clam liquor, water, pork pieces, onion, and potatoes. Cook this over low fire until potatoes are tender. Season with salt and pepper. Stir in the clams and milk. Cook for 10–15 minutes, stirring constantly. If desired, this may be thickened with a butter-flour paste made by creaming a small amount of flour to soften the butter. Blend in chowder slowly, stirring constantly. Ladle into soup platters, top with crumbled crackers, and place a pinch of finely chopped fresh parsley on top.

Baked Ham with Mustard Sauce (85¢)

10- to 20-pound ham
1 cup molasses
Whole cloves
Mint and pineapple for garnish

Preheat oven to 300°. Wash ham, place in a deep pan, and cover with cold water. Add a cup of molasses. Soak overnight. Next day, remove the skin and, with a sharp paring knife, make cross slits in the fat on the ham top. Stick a whole clove in the center of each square of cross slits. Place the ham in a roasting pan with a rack. Pour a small amount of water into the bottom of the roaster. Cover with a lid. Bake in the slow oven until brown, 25 minutes per pound. Remove from the roaster when done and garnish with mint and slices of pineapple.

Mustard Sauce

2 tablespoons butter
2 tablespoons flour
1½ cups brown stock
1 teaspoon prepared mustard
½ teaspoon salt

Dash pepper
1 teaspoon lemon juice

In a small saucepan, melt butter and blend in flour, stirring until bubbly. Add stock slowly, stirring continuously. When mixed, stir in mustard and seasoning. Mix well. When ready to serve, stir in lemon juice. The sauce may be poured over ham slices or served from a gravy dish.

Coffee and dessert were included as a "No Charge with Club Dinner" option.

Coffee Served with Bittersweet Chocolate–Peppermint Wafers

½ cup cold water
2 cups granulated sugar
2 squares bittersweet chocolate
¼ teaspoon cream of tartar
8–12 drops peppermint oil

In a medium saucepan, stir over a low heat water, sugar, chocolate, and cream of tartar. Heat while stirring until the sugar is dissolved and the chocolate melted. When the mixture begins to boil, place a candy thermometer in the pan and heat to 238° without stirring. Remove the pan from the heat and let it stand for 2–3 minutes. Add peppermint oil and beat candy until it is creamy and starts to cool. Immediately drop onto waxed paper, using a tablespoon. When hardened, place in tins with waxed paper separating the layers. Serve with after-dinner coffee on a doily-lined dessert dish.

It was at Schrafft's on Seventy-Third Street where Elizabeth renewed her friendship with college friend Betsy Helburn Strisower. Betsy, who had obtained her master's degree in nutrition at Columbia University, was now the dietitian for the Lebanon Hospital. Betsy remembered an event that took place during Prohibition, when Elizabeth had purchased a bottle of alcohol from a bootlegger. Betsy and Elizabeth were walking down Broadway when Elizabeth dropped the bottle, and it crashed to the ground at the feet of a police officer who was walking by. Betsy did not know where Elizabeth had purchased the booze, and in her panic, she quickly left her to deal with the dilemma and just kept on walking. This was a story that the two of them would laugh over for many years.

According to Betsy, Schrafft's advertised on their menu that they would please all their customers by honoring special requests of a patron's favorite food—whether it was on the menu or not— and most of the time, they succeeded. Elizabeth knew when Betsy had come into the restaurant because she would ask for something that was good, traditional Kentucky country cooking. All special orders had to be approved by the manager, and as soon as Elizabeth saw the request, she knew Betsy was there.

During this time, Elizabeth lived in a room in a large home on Riverside Drive. Her landlady rented old homes and operated them as boardinghouses. When the landlady decided to change her residence to a home on Broadway for larger quarters, her tenants went with her. Elizabeth was fortunate to live in beautiful old New York City homes.

Richard Ridgely, whose parents were from Cynthiana, was the financial backer for a restaurant chain in New York City called Ship Grill. Organizer and overseer of the Grill restaurants was Olin Potter. One of the managers was a young man from

Cynthiana, Clarence Lebus. Elizabeth received a dinner invitation to meet with the three men. They wanted her to come to work for them and to open a new Ship Grill in the basement of an apartment house on Fifty-Seventh Street. It would be hers to run exclusively, and the salary was on a percentage basis. The deal also included a free apartment in the building, with a fold-down bed.

Elizabeth had met Clarence Lebus a few years earlier in Cynthiana. He had come to an evening party given by her sister Lillie at the Cromwell house. Elizabeth prepared all the food for the party, and the menu included ribbon sandwiches. She used to jokingly say that her ribbon sandwiches must have left a lasting impression on Lebus.

Ribbon Sandwiches

Decide on the choice of bread for alternate layers: white, brown, rye, or whole wheat (commercial or homemade). Bread should be at least 24 hours old before cutting.

Slice the bread ¼ inch thick and trim the crusts from each side. The best utensil is a thin bread knife with a smooth edge. Use a gently sawing motion with a small amount of pressure to not tear the bread. While working with the bread and sandwiches, have slightly dampened towels to place over all food; this will keep the bread and sandwich spreads moist.

Be sure to spread a thin covering of mayonnaise on the inside of each bread slice before spreading the bread with sandwich spreads. Alternate white bread slice, sandwich spread, dark bread slice, sandwich spread, and white bread slice. Fix another set of sandwiches using dark bread slice, sandwich spread, white bread slice, sandwich spread, and dark bread slice.

When all sandwiches are assembled, cut each sandwich in thirds. Place on an attractive china platter, alternating bread colors around the platter. Cover with a dampened towel until ready to serve. Store in a cool place.

Olive Nut Spread

8 ounces cream cheese, softened
1 tablespoon mayonnaise
1 teaspoon olive juice
¼ cup Spanish olives with pimientos, chopped fine
¼ cup broken pecans, chopped

Stir cream cheese until smooth and creamy. Add a little mayonnaise and the olive juice to thin cream cheese. Blend in olives and nuts. Spread on bread to desired thickness.

Deviled Ham Spread

1 can deviled ham
Prepared horseradish
⅛ teaspoon onion, grated
Dash pepper

Blend all ingredients. Taste and increase seasoning to desired taste. Blend well. Spread evenly on bread.

Pimiento Cheese Spread

3-inch block American cheese
1½-inch block sharp cheddar cheese
2 whole pimientos, chopped
Mayonnaise

Grind or grate cheeses together. Blend slightly, adding pimientos. Add mayonnaise and blend to desired consistency. Spread thinly on bread slices.

Apricot Cream Cheese Spread

6 ounces cream cheese, softened
¼ cup apricot jam
2 tablespoons pecans, finely chopped

Combine cream cheese and apricots. Blend well. Stir in nuts and mix again. Spread thinly on bread slices.

Benedictine Spread

3 ounces cream cheese
2 teaspoons mayonnaise
½ teaspoon onion, peeled and grated
1 tablespoon cucumber, peeled and grated
2 drops green food coloring

Using the back of a serving spoon, cream the cheese. Add mayonnaise and blend until mixture is smooth. Add the coloring last. Stir together while counting to 100 to assure good blending. Store in a covered container overnight.

Quick Mayonnaise

½ teaspoon salt
Few grains of cayenne pepper
¼ teaspoon mustard
1 tablespoon apple cider vinegar
1 egg
1 cup olive oil, divided
Squirt of lemon juice

Mix dry ingredients; add vinegar and egg. Beat with eggbeater, add half of the oil, and beat until the mixture thickens. Add another ⅓ cup of oil and beat again until thick. Add the remaining oil and continue beating until thick. If the mixture becomes too thick, thin with lemon juice.

Elizabeth remembered the Ship Grill on Fifty-Seventh Street as feeling like home. Most of the residents ate at least one meal, if not three meals, a day in the restaurant. They had many drop-in customers, but the apartment tenants felt like family over time.

Keeping the menu interesting from day to day was a delightful challenge for Elizabeth. Ship's onion soup was one of her favorites.

Onion Soup

5 small onions, thinly chopped
3 tablespoons butter
6 cups brown stock
Salt to taste
6 slices, toasted French bread
3 tablespoons finely grated Parmesan cheese

In a large soup pot, cook onions in butter until soft. Add stock and salt. Simmer for 30 minutes. Place a slice of toasted French bread on each soup plate (toast should be cut to fit bowl size). Sprinkle it with cheese. Slowly ladle hot soup into bowls over bread. Top with additional grated cheese. Serve immediately.

Elizabeth's youngest brother, Jim, came to visit her in New York City. He was in the Ship Grill restaurant one day when the chef had become angry over events taking place in the kitchen. The chef grabbed his very expensive and well-honed knife set and burst from the kitchen in Elizabeth's direction to announce his departure from the job. Elizabeth's brother, unaccustomed to New York City's ways and temperamental chefs, rushed to protect his sister from the enraged chef by jumping in front of her. Elizabeth recalled this story with loving thoughts and said that the chef was so taken by surprise that the atmosphere calmed, and the problems were resolved.

When talking about the stock market crash in 1929, Elizabeth said that most people she knew were in complete shock. Many of those same people had not considered that the lifestyles they had become accustomed to could be threatened. When the crash came, everyone was worried, but, fortunately, people still needed to eat, and the restaurant had to adjust. Food supply costs came down, and the Ship Grill continued to feed people at a much lower cost so that their customers could afford meals.

In Kentucky, people were also still dining out. In Lexington, the Canary Cottage had become a popular restaurant. It was owned and operated by Richard M. Wheeler, better known as "Fish Wheeler," from Winchester, Kentucky. Richard Wheeler opened another Canary Cottage at 621 South Fourth Street in downtown Louisville, Kentucky. Both restaurants were thriving. They were doing so well that Wheeler wanted to open another Louisville restaurant in a new office building being constructed at Fourth and Broadway called the Heyburn Building. Wheeler traveled to New York City to entice Elizabeth Cromwell to return to Kentucky. Elizabeth's mother Eva had died in the fall of 1929, and she wanted to be closer to her family. So when Wheeler offered her a fifty-fifty percentage, she gave Potter her notice after three years at the Ship Grill.

French Village

Today's Special

Southern Corn Fritter

MAPLE SYRUP, CRISP BACON, NEW BEETS & PEAS

& Cole Slaw

Hot Rolls, Corn Sticks & Butter

35c

French Village flier, from Elizabeth Kremer's personal papers, 2016ms043.

In March 1930, Elizabeth Cromwell opened the French Village in the basement of the Heyburn Building. According to an article in the March 16, 1930, *Courier-Journal*, the main room was meant to look like a village in France and was built around an old stone drinking well. Each private dining room was a replica of an individual shop or café, with provincial style throughout. The French Village was in downtown Louisville's business hub, and there were executives to impress and society women to please. Elizabeth was ready to direct, and restaurant service was her specialty. This is how she translated that service model to the public: Elizabeth referred to dining as a performance for the customers.

> The guests who come to dine are wanting the best show for their money. It is going to take hostesses, waitresses, cooks, and busboys to please them. Each guest may be expecting something different from the show, so a complete knowledge of service should be known by the performers.

> Costumes are selected; appearance is very important. The outfit should be well fitted to all figures. This will designate the employee from others in the room and please the guest.

> Clothing should be clean, free of spots, and pressed daily. Hair and nails should be nicely done. Shoes should be sensible and in style with the costume but comfortable, because feet do get so very tired in restaurant work.

> Table service setup should include two teaspoons, knife, salad fork, and dinner fork.

> The waitress should be very familiar with the menu of the day before asking for an order. If the guest should have any questions of which the waitress is not sure, the

kitchen should be checked with for information before the order is taken. If there are any special dietary needs, the manager should be notified.

On entering, the guests should be treated as if they were the most important persons that have entered the door. Never should they be rushed or even made to feel they are being rushed. Your guests are seated and it's showtime. They should be smoothly, quietly, and quickly entertained.

The waitress should remember that "wait on" means to be at rest in expectation until the duties and supplies of the table are known.

It should be remembered that gratuities mean a feeling of being grateful, pleased, or thankful, and the word *TIPS* was interpreted as "to insure proper service." This means the waitress must earn the guests' approval and perform to their approval. Therefore, a pleasant time will be had by ALL.

Elizabeth loved to recall one great performance. A regular breakfast customer of the French Village requested the same order at every visit: coffee with cream, orange juice, boiled three-minute egg, toast, and grape jelly. He wanted a particular table every time he came in, which meant he would have the same waitress each time. She had learned his choices and food style, and she also knew what he really wanted. He wanted a five-minute egg, where the white was solid and the yellow thickly runny, and not a three-minute one. All was well unless that waitress had the day off. In that case, he would order his three-minute egg from the substitute waitress and then promptly send it back to the kitchen for another egg cooked "correctly." Elizabeth tried to convince the substitute waitress that the customer is always right, even when they are wrong. In this particular case, the customer wanted a three-minute egg cooked for five minutes.

Even though some Louisville banks were failing around the time the French Village opened and the Great Depression was working its way across the nation, people were still dining out. Food costs were at an all-time low, and the French Village was doing well.

Famous French Village Rolls

1 pound sugar
3 tablespoons salt
1 teaspoon baking soda
3 teaspoons baking powder
1 pound butter
1 pound lard
18 eggs
3 quarts milk, divided
½ pound yeast
11 pounds flour

Preheat oven to 350°. Mix sugar, salt, baking soda, baking powder, butter, lard, and eggs. Warm the milk, without boiling, and add the yeast to dissolve for about five minutes. Add the milk and yeast to the egg mixture then add flour gradually while mixing. Work dough until well blended. Form into a ball in a bowl. Cover with a damp towel. Pat out small amounts of dough on a floured surface, cut into round shapes, and place on a cooking sheet. Bake until golden brown.

Mary Hanson Peterson (better known as "Cissy" Gregg), around 1924 when she was a University of Kentucky undergraduate. UKL, Louis Edward Nollau F Series Photographic Print Collection, 1998ua001.

Mary Hanson Peterson, known as "Cissy," was one of Elizabeth's early friends in Cynthiana and at the University of Kentucky, where Cissy graduated in 1924 with a bachelor of science in agriculture. Classmates noted in the *Kentuckian* yearbook, "The world will be amply supplied with fresh fruit and a happy smile as long as Cissy has her 'Strawberry Acres.'" After working in extension and in other places, like Cincinnati, Cissy became the *Louisville Courier-Journal* home consultant. The newspaper carried her recipes and suggestions for over twenty years.

Cissy married Ed Gregg, a Louisville architect. He loved the beauty of nature, its hills and rivers. He had a bachelor friend who was a civil engineer who also loved nature. His friend also had a boat and a canoe to explore the Ohio River. Cissy invited Elizabeth to join the newlyweds and a few other friends on a short trip to one of the small islands on the Ohio River for an afternoon picnic. With Elizabeth's poor memory for names, she couldn't even remember her escort's name that afternoon, but she did remember the boat owner's name: Harold "Doc" Pemberton Kremer.

After this excursion, Doc went to Canada on a trip and left the care of his boat to his friends, who took advantage of its use during his absence. When Doc returned, he called on Elizabeth at the French Village, and that was the beginning of their relationship.

In 1932, Wheeler decided to expand his restaurant business again in downtown Cincinnati, Ohio. The new place was going in across from the Gibson Hotel, on 420–422 Walnut Street. Elizabeth Cromwell was off to Cincinnati to run the new business. Her relationship with Doc continued to grow during this time through letters and telegrams sent between the two cities. In one letter to Doc dated March 30, 1932, Elizabeth wrote how she got a most awful feeling in her tummy as opening day arrived, but she said, "I am trying to look very calm." According to the letter, "the store looks lovely, and the kitchen is perfect."

Interior view of the Canary Cottage dining room in Cincinnati, Ohio. UKL, Elizabeth Kremer Cromwell Papers, 2016ms043.

The Canary Cottage opened on April 12, 1932, on the ground floor of the Mercantile Library Building. It was divided into four public and four private dining rooms, each decorated with their own theme. The public dining rooms were known as the Cape Cod, Georgian, Connecticut, and Pioneer rooms. The private rooms were the Pine, Cincinnati, Old Kentucky, and Colonial rooms. The Depression worsened, but people continued to dine out in restaurants, and the cost of dining out continued to be low. Food costs from the suppliers were even lower, and the Canary Cottage in Cincinnati did well.

Pot Roast

The best choice of roast would be bladebone, shoulder, chuck, round rump, or sirloin tip.

    Salt and pepper
    ½ cup flour
    4- to 6-pound roast
    Hot fat
    ½ cup onion, chopped
    1 cup water
    10–12 new red potatoes
    4–6 carrots

Mix seasoning with flour. Dust and rub all sides of roast with the mixture. Melt fat in an iron skillet and sear all sides of the roast; this will help hold in juices. Place the onions, then meat and drippings in a large heavy kettle with a low rack on the bottom. This will keep meat from sticking and burning to the pan. Add water and a tight lid. Do not let the roast boil dry; add water when needed. Cook until tender but not flaky. As roast is cooking, peel and cut potatoes and carrots in large chunks; add them to the kettle during the last hour of cooking. A 3-pound roast should cook for 2–2½ hours; a 5-pound roast, 3½ hours. For larger boneless roasts, allow 1 hour more.

During this time, the need for civil engineers dwindled, and Doc Kremer lost his job. He left Louisville for Washington, DC, to visit and look for work for around a month. Unsuccessful, he returned to Louisville and went to work for the Ford Motor Company, where his job was to put on the left side of the hood. Ford insisted that its employees drive a Ford vehicle, so he purchased a Model T for twenty-five dollars. He was such a detail-oriented person that he was quickly promoted to timekeeper.

None of the uncertainty of the era prevented Doc from pursuing Elizabeth. Their courtship continued between Louisville and Cincinnati by car, bus, and train. They used telegrams to arrange pickup times. Many of Elizabeth's letters were written on the backs of menus; most were hastily written after shifts and related events that happened during business hours. Her letters often ended with endearments like "Would you like to know all you meant to me yesterday? Ask me some time, I haven't enough paper now. We don't buy menus by the thousands. Love, Elizabeth."

When Elizabeth did not write often enough, Doc would send a telegram, which she would finally answer by writing on the back of another menu. Even as some banks were closing due to the Depression and other banks were trying to hang on, the Canary Cottage continued to do well. Elizabeth often wrote to Doc about events that affected her employees. One such time, the bank contacted Elizabeth about one of her employees; they said that one of her waitresses had become hysterical over her money and requested that Elizabeth talk with her about her poor behavior. Elizabeth wrote to Doc about the incident, saying that the bankers seem awfully worried about what was happening to everybody else—meaning they should worry about their own industry rather than the behavior of her employees. On the back of another menu, she told a story about her cashier, Sidney, who had mistakenly accepted a counterfeit twenty-dollar bill, which prompted a call to federal agents. It doesn't seem that they impressed Elizabeth when the Secret Service man told her, "Well, don't you know, sister . . . it looks too good to be real." Her response to his rudeness: "Why do federal agents always have a tall and a short man, and is it a national law that one of them must smoke a cigar?"

During the temperance movement, Elizabeth's mother, Eva, marched in Cynthiana for the Woman's Crusade of 1873, a national movement whose impact reached Kentucky. Even so, Elizabeth herself was not opposed to drinking alcohol and enjoyed having a cocktail in the evenings. But Prohibition had kept restaurants from serving alcoholic beverages, so when it was over, operating a bar in the Canary Cottage was a new experience for Elizabeth. When Prohibition was repealed in 1933, Elizabeth had to deal with new liquor laws and pleasing the taste of the drinking public. In keeping with Elizabeth's approach to most things, she read up and kept a record of the more popular alcoholic beverages.

One side of the dining rooms at the Canary Cottage was remodeled and became the Steamboat Room. The walls were decorated with pictures of the Cincinnati Greene Line riverboats. Elizabeth claimed that adding bars to restaurants complicated their operations because you had to teach the staff how to handle intoxicated guests as well as screening the employees for potential drinking problems.

A letter to Doc after this stated, "Darling, I have spent an exhausting day trying to read the government liquor taxes, etc. I wish I had learned to read as you do instead of skimming along reading every third word. I don't know yet what it is all about."

> Canary Cottage Cocktails Quarter Hour
> Daily 4:45–5:00 p.m.
> Any cocktail—tall drink—spirits—wine or liquor $.25

Daiquiri

Bacardi (white label), 4 parts
Lime juice, 2 parts
Sugar, ½ part

Place ingredients in a cocktail shaker and add crushed ice. Shake vigorously for 3 minutes. Garnish glass with a pickled onion and serve with a cocktail napkin.

Mint Julep

Fresh sprig of mint
Bourbon, 2 parts
2 lumps of sugar, dissolved in a small amount of water

Dry a 7-ounce tumbler (preferably silver) thoroughly. Place a folded cloth napkin around the tumbler for insulation. Fill the tumbler with finely crushed ice. Place a sprig of mint on the inside of the tumbler. In a separate container, mix bourbon with the dissolved sugar and mix thoroughly. Pour over mint sprig and ice. Do not stir, and never crush the mint leaves against the tumbler.

Cheese Straws

¾ pound sharp cheese
1 small, rounded tablespoon butter
2 cups all-purpose flour
2 teaspoons salt
2 teaspoons dry mustard
½–1½ teaspoons red pepper

Preheat oven to 350°. Grate cheese. Let the cheese and butter stand until at room temperature. Mix thoroughly. Sift flour, salt, mustard, and red pepper into the cheese mixture. Work with your hands to form a dough ball. Place portions of dough into a cookie press, using a flat or star shape. Press onto an ungreased cookie sheet in rows. Bake for 10–12 minutes. Remove from the oven and cut in desired length. Return to the oven and continue baking for 10–15 minutes. Remove from the oven and cool. Store in tins.

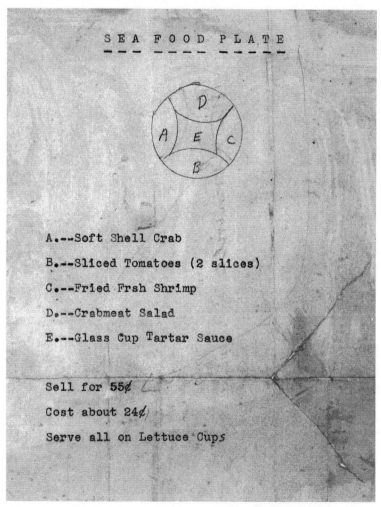

Elizabeth's original plating diagram for the seafood plate. UKL, Elizabeth Kremer Cromwell Papers, 2016ms043.

Elizabeth continued to excel in her professional life. In a memo from the main office in 1937, the Cincinnati Canary Cottage served 324,783 guests and had $207,266.84 in sales; food costs were 2 percent. She also continued to expect excellence among her staff. Elizabeth had rough sketches posted in the kitchen to make sure each food dish was correctly placed on the plate. Cooks, food checkers, waitresses, and busboys all knew what the dish should look like when it was served.

Soft-Shell Crab

Soft-shell crabs, 2 per person
Salt and pepper
Lemon wedges, 1 per crab
Fine bread crumbs
1 egg, beaten for every 2 crabs
Enough hot fat to deep fry

If crabs have not been cleaned, remove the spongy looking material from the underside of the body and gills. Remove eyes. Sprinkle with salt and pepper. Squeeze a lemon wedge over each crab. Dip the crabs in bread crumbs, then egg, and again in bread crumbs. Set aside to dry for about 20 minutes. Place crabs in hot fat with a slotted spoon. They will float to the top. When the edges of a crab look golden brown, turn the crab and cook a little longer until both sides are golden brown.

Crabmeat Salad

1 cup crabmeat, flaked
1 scant cup celery, finely chopped
¼ cup mayonnaise to moisten

Lightly toss ingredients together. Arrange on a lettuce leaf and top with a sprig of parsley.

Oyster Stew

3 cups milk
1 pint (16 ounces) fresh oysters and liquor
1 tablespoon butter
¼ teaspoon salt
¼ teaspoon celery salt
⅛ teaspoon black pepper

In the top pan of a double boiler, heat milk over boiling water until very hot. Strain oysters and preserve the liquor (approximately ¼ cup). In a shallow pan or skillet, melt butter, add oyster liquor, and heat until bubbling. Stir in seasonings. Pour oysters into bubbling mixture, stirring gently and continue cooking long enough for their edges to curl up. Remove from heat. (If oysters are very large, snip oyster into desired pieces with kitchen scissors.) Add this mixture to the hot milk. Pour into a large, rimmed soup plate. Place a butter patty or a small butter ball to float on top. Sprinkle on top a few grains of paprika to add color contrast. Place a serving plate beneath the soup plate and serve immediately. Place a small basket or shallow dish of oyster crackers to the upper left of the soup plate.

The Canary Cottage offered special dishes that were popular in other restaurants, and one of those was oysters Rockefeller. This dish was first served at Antoine's Restaurant, located in New Orleans, Louisiana, and was created by the chef and owner, Antoine

Blondeau. It was said that one guest to whom it was served exclaimed, "Rich as Rockefeller!" Antoine's oysters Rockefeller recipe is still highly sought after.

The dish was a favorite of many patrons, and oysters Rockefeller became common on the menus of many fine restaurants. Among Elizabeth's papers was the following recipe, sent from the main office to the Cincinnati location.

Oysters Rockefeller, Canary Cottage Style

2 dozen oysters in shell
Cooked bacon
½ teaspoon Tabasco sauce
1 tablespoon Worcestershire sauce
1 pint cream
1 cup fresh spinach, chopped
Grated Parmesan cheese

Preheat oven to 375°. Wash the oysters before shucking. Open with an oyster knife and remove the meat and the liquor into a bowl and set aside. Save one-half of the shell for each oyster. Place oysters back on the shell, adding a little liquor to each, and top each with a third of a piece of bacon. Put rock salt into pie pans and place each shell on top of the salt. The dish will be served hot in the baking dish. In a bowl, blend spicy sauces. Add cream and spinach. Toss this lightly until blended. Cover each oyster and lightly fill the shell with the mixture. Sprinkle the top with Parmesan cheese. Place pie pans in the hot oven and cook until the mixture is golden brown. Garnish with lemon slices and parsley. Serve immediately. The hot rock salt and oyster shell will help maintain the heat of the dish.

Old-Fashioned Potato Soup

8 boiling potatoes
2 cups hot milk
2 tablespoons butter
1 stalk celery, chopped
2 tablespoons chopped onion
1–2 teaspoons salt
½ teaspoon celery salt
¼ teaspoon black pepper

Boil potatoes with skin on until tender. Remove from heat and drain. Set aside until cool enough to handle. Remove the skin and cut into desired sized pieces. Heat milk in a double boiler to prevent scorching. In another saucepan place butter, stirring constantly, and then add celery, onion, salt, celery salt, and pepper. Simmer over low heat until celery has softened. Add potatoes and toss lightly to coat with seasonings. Slowly stir in hot milk and stir constantly to prevent sticking. Blend with the potato mixture. Serve in a large soup plate and garnish with a pinch of fresh chopped parsley.

Baked Bean Soup

3 cups cold baked beans (canned or leftover)
2 cups tomato puree
1 small onion, finely chopped
1 celery rib, finely chopped
4 cups hot water
1 tablespoon bottled chili sauce
Salt and pepper

2 tablespoons butter
2 tablespoons flour

In a large pot, combine the beans, tomato puree, onion, celery, and water. Cover and cook over medium heat for 30 minutes. Strain and force vegetables through a food mill or a strainer. Place the vegetable mixture in a soup pot and add chili sauce and seasonings. In a cup, combine the butter and flour and add enough water to make a smooth paste. Over low heat, add paste to the vegetable mixture, stirring constantly. Pour into wide-brimmed soup bowls and top with chopped parsley. Serve with Oertel's beer and a hot cheddar cheese sandwich.

Meat Loaf

2 eggs, beaten
½ cups tomato juice
½ cup chopped celery
1 small onion, minced
1 small green pepper, chopped
¾ pound ground beef
¾ pound ground veal
2 cups bread crumbs or cracker crumbs
2 teaspoons salt
¼ teaspoon ground pepper

Preheat the oven to 350°. Mix the eggs, tomato juice, celery, onions, and green peppers. Blend well. Mix this into the meat, stirring well to make sure the egg mixture covers all the meat. Add crumbs, salt, peppers, and blend well. Shape the meat mixture into a loaf and place in a heavy iron skillet or pan on a rack. Bake for 2 hours. Check the center with a fork to be certain the loaf is fully cooked.

Swiss Steak

½ cup flour
1 round steak (1½ or 2 inches thick)
Shortening or bacon fat
2 cups hot stock (2 cups water plus 2 beef bouillon cubes)
2 small onions
2 cups crushed tomatoes

Beat flour into steak with a meat hammer or ironstone china plate edge. Melt a small amount of shortening or bacon fat in a heavy iron skillet. When the fat is hot, brown floured meat on both sides. Pour stock and remaining ingredients over browned meat. Cover with a tight lid and simmer on stove top for 2 hours. Be sure to check at intervals to loosen the steak and keep it from sticking to the bottom of the skillet. A little water may need to be added during cooking time. Meat will tear apart easily with a fork when done. Serve in large pieces on a warmed dinner plate with a generous helping of cooked tomato sauce. Garnish with a sprig of parsley for color. Serve immediately.

Candied Sweet Potatoes

6 sweet potatoes
3 tablespoons butter
¾ cup brown sugar
1½ teaspoons fresh lemon juice
Dash of salt

Preheat oven to 350°. Boil sweet potatoes slowly in a large pan until tender. Set aside until cool enough to peel. Cut into ¼- to ½-inch slices and place in a shallow, greased baking dish. Dot potatoes with butter, sprinkle with brown sugar, lemon juice, and salt to taste. Cover and bake in oven for 10 minutes. Remove cover and continue cooking for 10–15 minutes more. Serve hot.

As a more formal dish, marshmallows may be added to the top of the potatoes, which can be returned to the oven long enough to puff and slightly brown the marshmallows. Small, individual ramekins may also be used, to be placed at the upper left edge of the dinner plate when an entrée has a thin gravy that would cover the plate.

Creamed Peas and Mushrooms

6-ounce jar sliced mushrooms
2 cups tiny, canned peas
2 cups heavy cream
2 tablespoons flour
¼ cup water
1 teaspoon butter
1 teaspoon salt
Dash red pepper

Drain mushrooms. In a large saucepan, heat peas slowly until hot; do not let them come to a rolling boil, as the peas will split apart. Drain peas and add mushrooms. Set aside. Place cream in a saucepan over low heat, stirring gently with a wooden spoon. Make a paste of the flour and water in a separate cup. When cream is hot, gently stir paste into cream. Continue cooking and stirring gently until cream begins to thicken. Stir in butter until melted. Add peas, mushrooms, and seasonings. Serve immediately.

Stewed Rhubarb

2 cups rhubarb
1 cup sugar

Wash fresh, red, small to medium rhubarb. Cut into ⅓- to ½-inch pieces. Place in a deep glass bowl and add sugar. Stir until the sugar is dissolved. Cover and stand for 12 or more hours. Place in a large saucepan and cook over very low heat. Simmer gently until rhubarb is tender, stirring occasionally to prevent sticking. Serve as a side dish with meat entree.

Banana Peanut Butter Salad

Bibb or leaf lettuce
½ banana
1 rounded tablespoon peanut butter
Peanuts, chopped
Mayonnaise

Wash and dry fresh crisp leaf or Bibb lettuce. Peel banana half. Place lettuce on a small salad plate and lay banana on lettuce. Spread peanut butter on top of fruit and sprinkle with nuts. Place a dollop of mayonnaise to the side of the banana and a small sprig of parsley on top of mayonnaise.

Cranberry Pineapple Congealed Salad

2 cups cranberries
½ cup crushed pineapple, drained
1 cup sugar
1 cup cranberry juice cocktail (divided into two, ½ cups)
1 envelope unflavored gelatin

Put cranberries through a food chopper. Blend pineapple with cranberries and mix well. Add sugar and mix until dissolved.

In a saucepan add half of the cranberry juice. Sprinkle gelatin on juice to soften. Place over low heat and stir until gelatin is dissolved. Remove from heat and stir in remaining juice. Blend this with cranberry mixture. Place in an oblong glass dish. Chill in the refrigerator until firm. Cut into squares and place on a salad plate on leaf lettuce with a dollop of mayonnaise. Garnish with a sprig of parsley.

Pecan Balls with Hot Fudge Sauce

Fresh, shelled pecan halves
French vanilla ice cream
Hot fudge sauce

Have waxed paper ready to roll around balls to place in the freezer. Lay out pecans in a shallow sheet-cake pan; this will allow you room to roll the ball and pick up the nuts on the surface of the ice cream. Let ice cream soften slightly. Scoop out a small (palm-sized) ball, coat with pecans, and wrap in waxed paper. Twist the end to keep airtight and place in the freezer until ready to serve. Hot fudge sauce may be made ahead, heated, and kept hot over low heat in a double boiler. When ready to serve, place balls in a shallow dessert dish. Add hot fudge sauce and a spoonful of unsweetened whipped cream, and balance a maraschino cherry with stem on top.

Hot Fudge Sauce

2 ounces unsweetened chocolate
1 tablespoon butter
⅓ cup boiling water

1 cup sugar

2 tablespoons corn syrup

1 teaspoon vanilla

Melt chocolate over boiling water. Add butter and stir until melted. Blend well. Stir in boiling water and mix well. Add sugar and syrup. Stir until sugar is dissolved. Place over low, direct heat and boil gently for 8 minutes. Do not stir. Add vanilla. Blend. May be stored in the refrigerator. Heat over boiling water before serving.

Piecrust

Double for a two-crust pie

1 cup flour

½ teaspoon salt

⅓ cup lard (if using shortening, use ⅓ cup plus

2 tablespoons)

2 tablespoons cold water

Place flour and salt in a dough bowl and mix lightly with your hands. Cut shortening into flour with a pastry cutter until it is the size of tiny peas. Sprinkle cold water over flour and begin mixing with a fork, stirring in a circular motion. As the mixture becomes stiff, use your hand to mix and knead until dough cleans sides of the bowl. Do not overwork, as this will make the crust tough. Roll out on a floured surface and put in a pie pan. If a single crust is used, flute edges with thumb and index finger and trim. If using a double recipe, do not flute until filling is in the bottom shell; then lightly dampen the rim of the bottom crust with finger and tap water. Place on top crust, press lightly around edge, and flute or pinch rim edge.

Pecan Pie

½ cup granulated sugar
1 cup corn syrup
3 eggs
1 teaspoon vanilla
¼ teaspoon salt
1 cup pecans

Preheat oven to 350°. Dissolve sugar in corn syrup. Beat eggs slightly. Stir in vanilla and salt. Blend well. Fold in pecans. Pour into a pie shell. Bake for 30–40 minutes. If piecrust seems to be getting too brown on the edges, lay a piece of aluminum foil lightly for the remaining cooking time.

Kentucky Sugar Pie

3 cups brown sugar
½ cup melted butter
½ teaspoon salt
3 eggs
½ cup single cream
1 teaspoon vanilla

Preheat oven to 325°. Beat ingredients together and pour into an unbaked pie shell. Bake in the slow oven for 30–40 minutes.

Simple desserts benefited from adding a high-quality maple syrup over French vanilla ice cream, and it was a big hit with patrons. The food costs were low, and the results were delicious.

Apple Dumpling

Piecrust
6 medium tart apples, cored
Brown sugar
Butter
Caramel Sauce

Preheat oven to 350°. Roll out a piecrust and cut into six 9-inch squares. Peel and core apples. Place each apple on a square of crust. Fill each apple center with brown sugar; dot with butter. Bring the sides of the piecrust up around the apple until it is completely covered. Place the dumplings in a shallow baking pan and bake for 30 minutes or until the fruit is tender. The crust should be lightly browned. Cool and serve with a caramel or hard sauce.

Caramel Sauce

1 cup brown sugar
½ teaspoon salt
1 tablespoon flour
1½ cups water
1 teaspoon butter
1 teaspoon lemon juice

In a small saucepan, mix brown sugar, salt, and flour until well blended. Add water, stirring constantly over low heat until sugar is dissolved. Bring to a boil. Stir in butter and lemon juice. Simmer for 5 minutes. Sauce may be served hot or cooled.

Hard Sauce

4 tablespoons butter, softened
1 cup confectioners' sugar
1 tablespoon fruit flavoring or liquor of choice

Cream butter and sugar. Add fruit flavoring, vanilla, rum, or brandy. Continue creaming until light in texture. If the sauce seems a little thin, add more sugar. For variety, a small amount of chopped nuts or coconut may be added.

The Canary Cottage menu had an open-faced grilled cheese and tomato sandwich on the menu for forty-five cents. Toast bread on one side. Place the bread; toast side down on a grill pan. Spread a thin layer of mayonnaise on the untoasted side of the bread. Place desired slices of tomato on the bread and arrange cheese slices over tomato slices, entirely covering the tomato. Place under the oven broiler and grill until the cheese has melted. Remove from the broiler and transfer to a dinner plate. Serve with potato chips and 4 apple wedges (with peel on) placed on a piece of Bibb lettuce.

The main office for the Canary Cottage restaurants was in Lexington, Kentucky. R. M. Wheeler would send daily memos by post from Lexington to his managers.

> Letter #48
> Lexington, KY
> August 20, 1937
> Attention Managers:
> Starting at once you will use the following for chicken dishes; would suggest you use only hens and turkey.
> For breast of chicken, use only white meat.
> For Chicken a la King, use the breast and thigh with fresh mushrooms.
> The legs and the rest of the chicken to be used for chicken croquettes, patties, cutlets, etc.

Chicken pot pies should have about 50% dark and 50% white meat with the giblets mixed with them.

Attention Managers:

I have ordered glass hens that are to be used in serving Chicken a La King, Creamed Chicken, etc. I think the size is exactly right for a nice serving and would suggest you run on the regular luncheon and dinner at 65 cents.

Eggs à la King

6 eggs
4 mushrooms, sliced
Butter
2 cups cream sauce
Salt and pepper to taste

Cook eggs to a hard-boiled stage and cool. When cooled, peel and cut into quarters. Set aside. Sauté mushrooms in one tablespoon of butter and set aside.

Basic Cream Sauce

2 tablespoons butter
2 tablespoons flour
Salt
2 cups cream (16 ounces)
Salt and pepper to taste

In a saucepan, melt butter over low heat. Stir in flour and salt. Stir constantly until blended well. When the mixture begins to bubble, slowly begin to pour cream into the saucepan. Bring to a boil and simmer for 2 minutes. Continue stirring and then remove from heat. When ready to serve, taste cream sauce for seasoning and add more if needed. Gently fold in mushrooms and eggs. Serve in tart shells or over crisp toast.

Creamed Chicken Mold

5-pound chicken (when cooked, it should yield 3 cups)
1 cup mushrooms, sliced
1 cup cream sauce, medium thickness
3 eggs
1 tablespoon butter, melted
2 teaspoons parsley, chopped
Salt and pepper to taste

Preheat oven to 400°. Grind cooked chicken and mushrooms together. In a large bowl, combine the cream sauce, chicken mixture, and the eggs. Using a beating stroke, mix these together. Blend in seasoning. Place in a mold or loaf pan that has been generously buttered. Cover with a lid or foil. Place this pan in a larger pan containing about ½ inch of water. Bake for 1½ hours. Serve with cream mushroom sauce.

Cream Mushroom Sauce

3 tablespoons butter
1 teaspoon grated onion
3 tablespoons flour
1 cup cream
½ pound mushrooms, sliced
Salt and pepper
Paprika

Over low heat, brown butter slightly in a saucepan. Stir in mushrooms, grated onion, and flour. Stirring constantly, cook until the flour is brown in color and mushrooms are tender. Continue stirring and blend in cream. Season with salt, pepper, and paprika.

Chicken à la King

⅓ cup butter
⅓ cup flour
1 cup chicken broth
1½ cups cream
1 cooked hen, meat removed and diced (when cooked,
should yield 3 cups)
1 cup mushrooms, sliced
1 pimiento, cut into strips
1 green pepper, cut into strips
1 teaspoon sherry
2 teaspoons salt
⅛ teaspoon pepper
Paprika and parsley to garnish

Melt butter on the top of a double boiler. Add flour and blend well.
Gradually add the chicken broth and cream. Stirring constantly,
cook until thickened. Fold in diced chicken, mushrooms, pimiento, green pepper, sherry, salt and pepper.

Sprinkle with a touch of paprika and a sprig of parsley. Place
in glass hens, pastry tart shells, or serve with griddle corn cakes
on a dinner plate.

Chicken Croquettes

Have ready a thick cream sauce; see recipe below.

2 cups cooked chicken, chopped
¼ teaspoon celery salt
½ teaspoon salt
½ teaspoon paprika
1 teaspoon parsley, minced
1 teaspoon grated onion

1 cup fine cracker or bread crumbs
1 egg, beaten with 1 tablespoon water
Oil for frying

Blend chicken and seasonings together. In a bowl combine chicken mixture and cream sauce. Chill in a shallow pan. When thoroughly cooled, form into cone shapes. Roll in crumbs and then in egg mixture. Roll again in bread crumbs. Let croquettes dry on a platter. Place 1½ inches oil in a heavy skillet and place over medium heat. When the oil is hot, place croquettes and cook to a golden brown, turning for even cooking. Drain on a towel. Top croquettes with a mushroom sauce or a rich, thick cream sauce.

Basic White Sauces

Thin

1 tablespoon butter
2 tablespoons flour
¼ teaspoon salt
2 cups cream
⅛ teaspoon pepper

Medium

2 tablespoons butter
2 tablespoons flour
¼ teaspoon salt
2 cups cream
⅛ teaspoon pepper

Thick

¼ cup butter
¼ cup flour

¼ teaspoon salt
2 cups cream
⅛ teaspoon pepper

Place a saucepan over low heat to melt the butter. Add flour, salt, and pepper, stirring constantly until it is bubbly. Add cream and continue stirring to prevent lumps from forming. Cook to desired thickness and remove from heat.

Sometime between 1934 and 1935, Doc Kremer asked Elizabeth Cromwell to marry him. He gave her a family diamond, to be placed in the ring setting of her choice. The Canary Cottage restaurant was doing well, and as a result, work was taking up a significant amount of Elizabeth's time—so much time that she found it difficult to make the time to travel to Louisville to meet with the family jeweler. Several appointments were made, and then the appointments were canceled. Not to be deterred, Doc set off to the Canary Cottage in Cincinnati with three jeweler trays of ring settings for Elizabeth to choose from. Meeting her on her time, Elizabeth was finally able to select a ring, and Doc returned to Louisville to have the diamond set.

From the Cynthiana Democrat March 2, 1935:

A wedding of interest to a wide circle of friends took place Saturday afternoon, March 2, at 3 o'clock, when Miss Elizabeth Cromwell and Mr. Harold Pemberton Kremer were united in marriage at the residence of the bride's father, the old Cromwell home on North Main Street. The marriage ceremony was said by the Rev. V. P. Merrell of the Presbyterian Church. It was a quiet affair, beautiful in its simplicity, only the members of the immediate families and a few close friends being present; the spacious rooms were beautifully decorated with masses of spring flowers, tulips, narcissi, sweet peas, and snapdragons. The attractive bride wore an exquisite gown of turquoise blue moss crepe, fur trimmed, and a shoulder bouquet of gardenias. She is the youngest daughter of John M. Cromwell and Eva Berry Cromwell. She was graduated from the Cynthiana High School and also from the University of Kentucky, where she was a member of the Kappa Kappa Gamma sorority. She is at present manager of the Canary Cottage in Cincinnati. Mr. Kremer is the only son of Dr. J. W. Kremer and Mrs. Eugenia P. Kremer, of Louisville. He received his training as civil engineer at the Rose Polytechnic Institute at Terre Haute, Indiana, and at present holds a position as engineer with the PWA in Lexington. He is a member of Theta XI fraternity. Following the ceremony, an informal reception was held. Refreshments of individual ices and cakes carrying out the color scheme of the flower decorations were served.

Doc had taken a job with the newly formed Public Works Administration. The government was helping to improve the economy by building roads, schools, and other public buildings. They needed engineers, so Doc was traveling often, and Elizabeth was busy feeding lots of hungry people in Cincinnati.

In January 1937, it began to rain. The Ohio River surged beyond its banks, and both Cincinnati and Louisville were hit by their worst flood in history. Doc was in Louisville, and Elizabeth was still in Cincinnati.

In a memo from Wheeler in Lexington: "Since Louisville and Cincinnati have reached the high-water mark, I would suggest that you watch all motors and see that the same is off the floor as much as possible—have someone watch them all night."

All the Canary Cottages suffered damage, but the French Village in Louisville was hit the hardest. Even so, Elizabeth had her restaurant back in order and reopened by February 20. The bad memories of the 1937 flood were quickly overshadowed for the Kremers, because in January, Elizabeth found out that she was going to have a baby later in June.

With the help of a live-in nurse, a brother, and a sister, Doc continued with the PWA, and Elizabeth went back to running the Canary Cottage after the birth of their daughter "Pem," Anna Pemberton Kremer, on June 14, 1937. Not only was Elizabeth a working woman, but she was a working mother. Elizabeth wasn't afraid to break norms, and she was ambitious. Courtship letters were replaced by snapshots and homemade movies along with family trips to the park or the Ohio River as well as celebrations of birthdays and holidays.

Elizabeth had been part of the US workforce since the 1920s, when only 20.3 percent of that workforce were women. By 1940, when Elizabeth stopped working, that number had only risen to 24.4 percent. She continued to work after she got married, also unusual for a woman during this time, and went back to work for three years after Pem was born. She'd had a successful sixteen-year career, lived in New York City, and ran many successful restaurants.

Despite all her success, in November 1940, Elizabeth gave notice to R. M. Wheeler that she was leaving the Canary Cottage because she was expecting her second child in February. She knew that with two children, it was time to devote more space to family and to raising their girls on Shady Lane in Louisville, Kentucky.

4

The Home Economist

This new phase of Elizabeth's life allowed her to be a full-time wife, mother, and homemaker. When old friends would ask her what she was doing now, Elizabeth would respond with delight and her usual sense of humor: "Oh, I'm just a housewife." Fortunately, Doc and Elizabeth complemented one another. She relied on Doc for his ability to remember names and dates, and he counted on Elizabeth for her social sense.

Doc was lively, athletic, and physically competitive. He had played football when he was younger and often complained that the sport was ruined for short men when clipping was outlawed. He gave instructions to both of his daughters on how to clip and break people's legs. Elizabeth, who was active in the UK Women's Athletic Association and an officer for campus women's soccer, disliked football's roughness but still attended the Male-Manual High School games in Louisville on Thanksgiving Day almost every year. It was the rivalry of the year for many of the alumni of the old high schools.

As a civil engineer, Doc loved structures, buildings, and bridges, and he enjoyed the practical aspects of the profession. Even when he was debilitated with arthritis and had to use a cane, he insisted on doing his own surveying. Elizabeth considered bridges something that you crossed and buildings as places to do things in. The two loved each other deeply but had lively differences. When they had a disagreement, the two fought as they lived—idiosyncratically, intensely, and with much flair.

They seldom disagreed about food, except that he disliked country ham and lamb fries (two of Elizabeth's favorites), and she disliked pickled pig's feet (one of his favorites). Even still, if they were at a restaurant that served either country ham or lamb fries, Doc would order it for her. With her restaurant background, Elizabeth often experimented with recipes. Sometimes she was more "innovative" than Doc liked, but even then, his most critical statement was "Well, this was all right for a change." With that, she knew he didn't care for it and rarely prepared the recipe in that way again. As the social expert, Doc let Elizabeth pick the restaurants when the family traveled. Often they would eat a light breakfast in the motel room to save money so that they could spend more on the most highly recommended restaurant in town.

Elizabeth was the one who knew food, but Doc often made suggestions. Doc was the one who knew about driving and geography, but still Elizabeth often made her own suggestions. Typically, they ignored each other's "suggestions" in their respective fields of expertise. Two things that Doc and Elizabeth never agreed about were the weather and religion. Doc loved violent changes in weather, which Elizabeth feared. He had always wanted to see a tornado and often relished his memories of the 1937 flood. Elizabeth was a member of the Presbyterian church, but Doc never joined. He would often drive her to church, sit through the sermon, but wait in the car if there was a meeting after.

Doc was a musician, specifically a pianist, and he loved musical theater, opera, and the Louisville Philharmonic. The family had season tickets to Louisville's outdoor amphitheater in Iroquois Park. Elizabeth loved musical theater and quiet music. Doc liked those, too, but he also liked opera and Bach. When he was angry with Elizabeth, he would storm to the piano and play either the triumphal march from Aida or a selection from Bach as loud as possible. In the summer, Elizabeth would quietly go around the house pulling down the windows so that his loud playing would not disturb the neighbors.

When Elizabeth resigned from the Canary Cottage in Cincinnati, they moved into a home on Shady Lane off Eastern Parkway in Louisville, in an area known as the Highlands. The backyard of the house connected with the backyard of an old college friend, Marion Seegar Campbell, and her husband, Henry—or Miss Dutch and Humpy, as they were known to the family.

Having good friends as neighbors was very convenient and gave Doc a sense of security, as he was still frequently traveling with his job. He liked having people he could trust close by, since Elizabeth was due with their second child. On February 12, 1941, Evalina Cromwell Kremer, named after Elizabeth's mother, was born. Elizabeth was thirty-nine when Evalina came; she would joke that she had to ask the doctor, "Am I too old to have a baby?" She said later that what she should have asked was "Am I too old to raise a baby?" However, Elizabeth had no trouble breaking norms, whether it was being an active and successful woman in the workforce or challenging age stereotypes.

Much like their unconventional courtship, Doc and Elizabeth both actively raised their girls. The birthdays were ceremonially celebrated with birthday cakes on dining tables laid out with the proper table settings and a pair of silver candlesticks, of course. Doc was still traveling a great deal with the US Housing Authority, and letters came regularly from Washington, DC, where he spent two months. When jobs were closer to Louisville, the family would go and stay wherever he was working. Many old Kentucky hotels were the background of family photos showing Pem and Evalina on their porches.

Elizabeth didn't spend much time improving her handwriting, and the daughters learned early on how to translate some of her scribbles. The US Post Office tried to interpret Elizabeth's handwriting when she was keeping in touch with her traveling husband during the wartime. One of his letters contained the following message:

> Dear Elizabeth, I am enclosing the envelope of your letter so that you can see what happens to a letter when the address is not written so that you can tell what it is. I did not receive the letter until this morning.
>
> Notice the memoranda on the back of the envelope. It went to "L" and then "S" and the "G" was the last guess, and it certainly was not the logical one.
>
> In this particular instance I do not see why they did not check up on the Columbia Hotel, but you know in assorting the mail they only look at the city and on the receiving end only at the street.
>
> In any case, you should check the address before you mail it, especially if it is important. You should make the "G" a printed one, as I have checked your other letters and 75% of them look like a "S."

From the fall of 1941 until 1942, Doc and Elizabeth and their two daughters moved around a lot. After the bombing of Pearl Harbor, their addresses included St. Albans, West Virginia, and Hampton Roads, Virginia, and by December 1942, they were residing in Edgewood, Maryland.

An engineering coworker, Christy Christianson, requested that Doc be assigned to Edgewood to work on the housing project there. In a letter thirty years later, Christy stated what a good fortune it was to have Doc with him: "As part of my crew, we worked together as a team and produced projects for our county in record time and at a savings in cost below budget and in doing so contributed in no small way to the War Effort."

Elizabeth had a victory garden behind their duplex in the housing project where they lived in Edgewood. Like many Americans during this time, Elizabeth did her part to reduce their reliance on commercial food during rations. She was very proud of her garden and developed many recipes in which to use the vegetables. These remained on the family's menu through the years. They loved fresh spinach, cooked quickly and served with sliced hard-boiled eggs. Elizabeth presented this vegetable dish on the table with a small, handblown, blue glass vinegar bottle with a glass stopper. The children were allowed to add their own apple cider vinegar to their spinach, and it felt like such a grown-up thing to do.

Green beans from the garden were cooked slowly for hours with a smoked ham hock, the cheapest meat from the grocery. Fresh, sliced carrots were boiled until tender and a buttery brown sugar glaze with a pinch of chopped fresh parsley was put on them just before being served. The children loved the carrots. The girls remembered Elizabeth's vegetable soup being so good. It was also very inexpensive, which was important during this time.

Meatless Western Vegetable Soup

1 quart water
2 quarts fresh tomatoes, peeled and chopped
2 potatoes, peeled and diced
1 small onion, finely chopped
2 teaspoons salt
2 cans kidney beans
2 stalks celery, finely chopped
2 carrots, sliced

1 clove garlic, chopped
1½ teaspoons sugar
2 tablespoons chili powder
½ small head cabbage, chopped

Place all ingredients in a large soup pot and bring to a boil, stirring often to prevent sticking. Reduce heat to low and simmer for 2 hours.

Victory Garden Salad

Plant assorted spring lettuces. When ready, pull leaves in the morning. Wash, shake, and place in the refrigerator between linen dish towels until ready to use. Cut a small handful of chives; wash and finely mince. Thinly slice a couple of radishes, grate a fresh carrot, sprinkle with prepared garden vegetables and top with a sprig of parsley. Serve with homemade French dressing or a daub of mayonnaise.

Summer Vegetable Molded Salad

¼ cup cold water
1 envelope unflavored gelatin
1 cup hot water
¼ cup sugar
½ teaspoon salt
1 tablespoon lemon juice
¼ cup vinegar
¾ cup celery, diced
¼ cup cucumber, diced
½ cup carrots, grated
2 teaspoons onion, grated
2 tablespoons green pepper, finely chopped

Place cold water on the top of a double boiler, sprinkle gelatin on the water and dissolve. Place the pan over boiling water and stir in hot water, sugar, and salt. Stir over heat until dissolved. Add lemon juice and vinegar. Remove from heat and chill until the consistency of egg whites. Mix in the remaining ingredients and pour into a large mold or individual molds. Place in the refrigerator until set. Serve on lettuce leaves with a touch of mayonnaise on top and a sprinkle of paprika.

Sauerkraut

2 large heads cabbage
3 scant tablespoons salt

Chop or shred cabbage and place in a large crock. Toss cabbage lightly while adding the salt. Press down into the crock until a briny juice forms. Place a clean cloth over the top. Put a flat lid on top and add a weight of some kind to keep the cabbage compact. Ten days later, skim and pack kraut tightly in quart jars and seal. It's best to have an area outside the kitchen as this mixture begins to ripen.

Spareribs and Sauerkraut

2 tablespoons fat
2 pounds pork spareribs
2 teaspoons salt
2 teaspoons garlic powder
⅛ teaspoon pepper
2 cups water
1 quart sauerkraut

In a heavy-bottomed pot or Dutch oven, melt the fat. Cut spareribs in pieces that will permit browning in melted fat. Sprinkle with seasoning on both sides. Brown each piece on both sides in melted fat. When all pieces are browned, place all the meat in the bottom of the pot and add water. Cover and simmer over low heat for 2½ hours. Add a small amount of water if necessary. When meat is tender and falling away from the bone, add sauerkraut. Cover again and cook until the kraut is hot.

Elizabeth was constantly budgeting because of food rationing, so she tried new recipes quite often. Spam was something the children liked, and sometimes she would fry it and serve it as a warm sandwich, but other times she would give them something different. Even Spam was never plain or ordinary in the Kremer household. Spam was shelf-stable and budget-friendly, and it surged in popularity after its release in 1937, particularly during and after World War II.

Baked Spam with Pineapple Slices

1 can Spam
1 can sliced pineapple
Maraschino cherries
Fresh-squeezed orange juice
1 teaspoon brown sugar per meat slice

Preheat oven to 350°. Slice Spam to desired thickness. Place Spam slice in a shallow glass baking dish. Put ½ pineapple ring on each Spam slice. In the half circle, place a sliced cherry. Dribble about a tablespoon of orange juice over the cherry and pineapple slice. Sprinkle brown sugar over each meat slice; bake for 10–15 minutes. Serve immediately.

Spam Pancakes

1 egg, beaten
1¼ cups buttermilk
2 tablespoons oil
1¼ cups flour, sifted
1 teaspoon sugar
2 teaspoons soda
1 teaspoon baking powder
2 teaspoons salt
1 can Spam, cut into ¼-inch slices

Break egg into a large mixing bowl and beat with a rotary beater. Add milk and oil and beat well. Beat in dry ingredients until smooth. Place Spam on a hot, greased griddle, allowing space for pancake batter to form a cake. Most griddles will allow for 4. Fry Spam for a few seconds on one side and turn. Spoon enough batter on the Spam slice to form a 3-inch round cake. Grill slowly until bubbles appear in the batter and edges are golden brown. Flip pancake and continue to grill until both sides are golden brown. Top with melted butter and hot maple syrup.

Creamed Spam and Eggs

3 eggs, hard-boiled
1 can Spam, diced
2 tablespoons butter
2 tablespoons flour
2 teaspoons salt
Dash of pepper
1 cup milk

Cook eggs to a hard boil, remove shells, and slice. Set aside. Dice Spam and set aside. Melt butter in a saucepan, add flour, salt, and pepper, stirring constantly, and cook until mixture is bubbling. Slowly stir in milk. Continue stirring until mixture begins to thicken. Fold in Spam and stir gently as it heats. Add sliced eggs. Serve on a slice of thin toast, or serve in a split baked potato.

Spanish Rice

1 cup rice
2 tablespoons salad oil
2½ cups peeled, diced tomatoes
1 tablespoon salt
¼ cup green pepper, chopped
½ cup onion, chopped
4 cups boiling water
1 tablespoon chili powder

Wash rice and place in a heavy-bottomed pot. Add the remaining ingredients. Cook over low heat, stirring occasionally for 30–40 minutes or until rice is tender.

Navy Bean Soup

16 ounces dried navy beans
Water
2 medium onions, chopped
4 stalks celery, chopped
1 ham hock
⅛ teaspoon pepper
2 teaspoons salt
1 carrot, diced

Soak beans overnight in enough water to cover 1 inch above the beans. Drain and sort over to remove the bad beans and half pieces. Chop onion and celery. Place all ingredients in a large soup pot. Add enough water to measure 2 inches above the beans. Bring to a boil over high heat, stirring occasionally. Reduce heat and simmer for 2 hours. (The children preferred this dish to be served with a ketchup bottle on the table.)

One of the children's favorite cookies was gingerbread boys. Elizabeth would let the girls help with sprinkling the granulated sugar and placing the red dots for the eyes.

Gingerbread Boys

1 cup shortening
1 cup sugar
1 egg, slightly beaten
1 cup molasses
2 tablespoons vinegar

Sift together

5 cups all-purpose flour
½ teaspoon salt
1 teaspoon ground cinnamon
1½ teaspoons baking soda
2–3 teaspoons ground ginger
1 teaspoon ground cloves

Preheat oven to 375°. Cream shortening with sugar until dissolved. Stir in egg, molasses, and vinegar and blend well. Add sifted ingredients. Blend this into the molasses mixture. Chill for 3 hours. On a lightly floured surface, roll dough ⅛ inch thick. Cut with gingerbread cutter. Place 1 inch apart on a greased cookie sheet. Use red-hot candies for the face and buttons. Bake in the moderate oven for 5–6 minutes. Makes 5 dozen.

This may be decorated with confectioners' sugar icing (but the girls preferred it without).

Chocolate Chunk Squares

At this time, chocolate was packaged as a segmented bar to be broken apart in ounces. To have the pieces called for in this recipe it was necessary to cut them on a cutting board with a chipping knife, so that some pieces were small and some large.

1 (7-ounce) semisweet chocolate bar
2¾ cups flour, sifted
2½ teaspoons baking powder
½ teaspoon salt
⅔ cup shortening
2¼ cups brown sugar
3 eggs
1 cup pecans, broken
1 teaspoon vanilla

Preheat oven to 350°. Cut the chocolate bar into small pieces with a chopping knife. Mix and sift the flour, baking powder, and salt. Melt the shortening and stir in the brown sugar; stir until well mixed. Allow to cool and add eggs one at a time, beating after each addition. In a large mixing bowl, slowly blend in dry ingredients. Stir in the nuts, chocolate, and vanilla. Place batter in a well-greased, oblong pan. Bake for 35 minutes. Makes 3 dozen squares.

Bowen Lee was a fellow engineer at the Edgewood project. Bowen was born in San Francisco, but his parents had immigrated from China. His wife, Kam Ngit (Rita, to the family), was born in Honolulu. Rita's parents were raised in Hawaii but were born in China. Bowen was sent to China in 1938 by the US government for some engineering duties related to the war in Europe. Rita was in college in China when they met and then got married.

The Lee family, Bowen, Rita, and their daughter Bunny were neighbors of the Kremer family in the Edgewood housing project. Bowen and Doc had engineering in common and became great friends. Elizabeth and Rita bonded over their love of cooking and became close friends.

Elizabeth loved Rita's dishes and was in awe that the only kitchen implements Rita used were chopsticks and a meat cleaver. Rita said that her family celebrated special holidays with lots of recipes handed down over the years, and her cooking skills were incredible.

Many years later, the Lee family visited the Kremers in Louisville, and Rita was featured in Cissy Gregg's food section of the *Courier-Journal*, which included the following recipe for a nice complexion.

Rita's Healthy Complexion Rice

Wash rice well in a bowl of water, rubbing the rice between the hands. Drain. Wash the rice a second time but save the water and drink it after draining it off the rice. Wash the rice a third time and drink the water again. This water is good for the system, but it is the second rinsing that really counts for the complexion. After the third washing, place the drained rice in a cooking vessel deep enough so that pointing straight down with your forefinger over the rice, the fingertip should just miss the top of the rice. Add water until it comes up to the first joint of the finger. Heat over high heat until the water boils and then reduce the temperature. Simmer until tender.

Chinese Spareribs

2 cups soy sauce
2 cups sugar
4 pounds spareribs, cut into riblets
Dash of cinnamon

In the morning, blend the soy sauce and sugar together. Place ribs in a container and douse meat with the sauce. Cover tightly and store in the refrigerator. Turn frequently throughout the day. Preheat the oven to 300°. Place the ribs in a drip pan and pour the sauce over the ribs. Sprinkle the meat with ground cinnamon. Bake in the slow oven for 2–3 hours or until crispy. Baste often with the drippings from the bottom of the pan.

When Rita fixed a chicken, she used as many parts as possible. She was deft with her meat cleaver, and this is what she used to cut up her bird.

Chicken Wings, Neck, and Back

Place wings, neck, and back in a large pot of water. Simmer for 6 hours. Strain and discard the chicken parts. Use stock for soup.

Chicken Breasts

The chicken breasts should be slivered and cooked quickly in a small amount of peanut oil in a shallow skillet. Diced asparagus, thinly sliced, with Chinese celery, fresh mushroom, and slivered almonds should be added halfway through the cooking time. The chicken and vegetables should be served over rice.

Chicken Legs and Thighs

1 cup soy sauce
1 cup peanut oil
2 cups sugar
2 cups water
Dash of ground ginger
Chicken legs and thighs

Combine the first five ingredients and blend well into a sauce. Place legs and thighs in a shallow pan or wok. Pour sauce over chicken. Cover and cook slowly until tender. Remove from the pan and separate meat from the bone. Cut the chicken into small slices. Return the chicken to the skillet and turn off the heat. Let it stand until ready to serve and then reheat. Serve with rice.

Chicken Giblets

Chop the giblets into small pieces and cook with fresh, snapped green beans. Season with salt, pepper, and a dash of ginger. Cook until done.

In 1945, the Kremer family returned to Louisville, Kentucky, when Doc got a job with the construction firm of Sullivan and Cozart. The family moved into Dr. John William Kremer's former home at 1830 West Jefferson Street. John Kremer, Doc's father, had owned a medical practice that he ran out of his house.

Dr. Kremer passed away while the family was in Edgewood, but the estate had not been settled because of the war.

John Kremer was the only one of his siblings to be born in the United States when the family came to America from Stuttgart, Germany. His German heritage was passed on through the family with food. Both Elizabeth and Doc held special family connections to food.

In Louisville, Pem attended fourth grade at Shawnee Elementary School, and Evalina went to kindergarten at the age of five. The family was able to settle Dr. Kremer's estate and sold the home on Jefferson Street. The family then moved to the west end of Louisville, into an apartment complex that had also been part of the estate. The apartment building on 614 South Forty-Second Street was two blocks from one of Louisville's many parks, Shawnee Park. During this time, Elizabeth oversaw church lunches and suppers as a member of the Third Presbyterian Church on Broadway. The recipes that she made for these luncheons and suppers were numerous, and the kitchens were places of great fellowship.

On Saturdays or some Sundays, the family would often take an afternoon drive to one of the beautiful parks in Louisville. Cherokee Park was one of Doc's favorites because of its many winding roads. He would drive by and admire the variety of nature's beauty especially the Tree of the Three Sisters. This was a tree with three main trunks growing out from the same root base. When persimmons were ripe, he would stop and pick one or two just to show the children what the "persimmon pucker" meant. They were so sour and left a lasting impression on the girls.

Doc loved the German recipes his paternal grandmother, Caroline Heckel Kremer, had made, and he often mentioned to Elizabeth that he wanted those dishes. As a woman who derived pleasure in cooking for her friends and loved ones, Elizabeth found her own method to prepare some of the comfort foods from Doc's family. German potato salad was one that she prepared often, and she wanted it to be as good as his grandmother's recipe. She often remarked that she knew it wasn't the same, even though Doc never complained.

German Potato Salad a la Elizabeth C. Kremer

8 medium boiling potatoes
4 strips of bacon
1 small onion, chopped
2 teaspoons cornstarch
4 teaspoons sugar
1 cup water
1 cup vinegar

Wash the potatoes and put in a large pot with water to cover. Cook until tender. Drain off water and cool slightly before removing the skins and slicing. In a heavy skillet, fry the bacon to a limp stage. Remove and place on a towel to dry. Chop in small pieces. In the leftover bacon grease, sauté the onion until tender but not brown. Add cornstarch, stirring constantly with a flat spatula. Stirring slowly, gradually add the sugar, water, and vinegar. Cook until smooth. Add potatoes and bacon. Gently toss to coat potatoes with the vinegar mixture. Cover and let stand until ready to serve. Potato salad may be served hot or cold.

Several years later, the family located Caroline Heckel Kremer's cookbook, written in German. The translated recipe is as follows.

Sour Potatoes

4 teaspoons sugar
¾ cup apple cider vinegar
8 strips of thick bacon
1 small onion, chopped
6–7 potatoes, peeled and sliced
1 teaspoon salt
1 teaspoon black pepper

Dissolve sugar in the vinegar and set aside. Fry the bacon in a large skillet until done, but not too crisp, adding the onion toward the end of the cooking. Add sliced potatoes and water to the skillet and season with salt and pepper. Cover with a tight lid and continue cooking on low heat, occasionally tossing gently with a flat spatula to ensure even coating of the potatoes. When the potatoes are tender, add the vinegar mixture. Continue cooking until the vinegar is hot, and serve warm.

The Kremer family continued to have a small garden out behind the apartment complex in Louisville. Evalina would cut chives from the garden for Elizabeth's version of Schmierkase, or spreadable cheese. Doc loved trying to teach his wife and daughters how to say the word properly, and the girls loved spreading the cheese on thick slices of dark rye bread fresh from the bakery.

Schmierkase

1, 6-ounce container of cottage cheese
⅛ teaspoon fresh garlic, minced
1 tablespoon fresh chives, minced
2 teaspoons fresh onion, grated

Place cottage cheese in a mixing bowl. Beat for 4 minutes until it thickens and the curd is very small. Beat in remaining ingredients and then let stand in the refrigerator overnight. Spread on pumpernickel bread or eat with a spoon.

All the Kremers loved sauerkraut and joked that it was in their "genes." Elizabeth's menus often included the sour cabbage as a main dish or a side salad.

Sour Cabbage

2 cups sauerkraut, drained
1 large green pepper, seeded and sliced thin
1 large onion, sliced thin
2 cups salad oil
2 cups cider vinegar
1 cup sugar

Place vegetables in a container that has a tight lid and set aside. Combine oil, vinegar, and sugar in a small saucepan. Heat over medium, stirring constantly until it boils. Pour this mixture over the vegetables, and let them stand in the refrigerator overnight. Occasionally open the container and press down on vegetables with a spatula to help soak all the vegetables. Serve cold.

German baked goods were also delicious, and at the time, every Old Louisville neighborhood had a corner bakery. Bakeries weren't open on Mondays but always on Sunday; no blue laws restricting work would stop them.

Ruth Ann Bakery was located at 4223 Vermont, a short two blocks from the family's apartment. On Saturday mornings before breakfast, the girls were allowed to go and purchase *kuchen* (German word for yeast cake). The cake would be loosely wrapped in white pastry paper and tied with thin string. The girls would carry it home, holding it flat to make sure the toppings stayed intact. Cinnamon kuchen was the girls' favorite cake. They particularly liked it when their father would go with them and they would bring back peach or apple kuchen with icing, butter kuchen, and cinnamon kuchen. Elizabeth seemed to think this was excessive but only ever said, "Oh, Doc."

Cinnamon Kuchen

This recipe makes two 8-inch or 9-inch cakes
2 pounds butter
2 cups granulated sugar
1 cup cold milk
1 cake of fresh yeast (2¼ teaspoons active dry yeast)
4½ cups all-purpose flour
1 teaspoon salt
3 egg yolks, beaten
Cinnamon topping

Cinnamon Topping

2 cups brown sugar, firmly packed
1½ teaspoons cinnamon
4 tablespoons flour
2 tablespoons butter, melted

Melt butter over low heat and then add sugar and milk. Heat this mixture until warm but not hot. Add the yeast and remove from heat, letting stand for 3 minutes. Whisk flour and salt in a large bowl and add the yeast mixture once it's bubbly. Add beaten eggs and mix well. Pour into two well-greased cake pans, spreading evenly. Cover and let rise in a warm place (around 80°) until nearly double in size. Preheat oven to 350° and make the cinnamon topping. Mix topping ingredients together with your hands, being careful not to overblend. The mixture should be crumbly in appearance. Sprinkle over the top of the risen dough before baking. Bake for 30–45 minutes or until the edges of the kuchen are a light golden brown and then cool on wire racks for 10 minutes.

When the Christmas season approached, Ruth Ann's began having springerle and pfeffernuesse. These cookies were made early in December and stored in tins to age; the harder they got, the better the Kremer family liked them. Doc trained the girls in the art of cookie dunking. He used his coffee, and the girls dunked their cookies in warm milk. Elizabeth would give her family disapproving looks for dunking the cookies, but she still supplied the coffee and the milk. Christmas also included a tangerine in the toe of the girls' stockings that would hang from the fireplace mantle.

Pfeffernuesse

2 cups candied fruit
1 teaspoon lemon rind
1 teaspoon ground cloves
1 teaspoon ground cardamom
1 teaspoon nutmeg

3 teaspoons ground cinnamon
¼ teaspoon black pepper
1 teaspoon salt
1 teaspoon baking soda
¼ cup butter
2½ cups confectioners' sugar, sifted
6 large eggs
5 cups all-purpose flour

Chop the fruit and lemon rind very finely. Blend the chopped fruit and rind with the spices, salt, and baking soda. Cream the butter and sugar well with an electric mixer. Beat in eggs and mix well. By hand, stir in flour, small amounts at a time. Chill the dough. Shape into ¾-inch balls and place on an ungreased cookie sheet. Let sit for 8–12 hours at room temperature. Preheat oven to 300°. Turn the balls over and bake for 15–20 minutes.

Baked cookies can be rolled in confectioners' sugar, or a thin icing (made from hot water mixed with confectioners' sugar) can be dropped on each cookie. Let dry and store cookies in tins. The cookies are better if they are allowed to age.

Springerle

6 eggs
3 cups granulated sugar
1 teaspoon baking soda
6–8 drops anise oil
6½ cups flour

Beat eggs until light and then slowly add sugar. Add baking soda and anise oil; blend well. Beat at medium speed for 15 minutes. Begin adding flour, but as the dough begins to thicken, work the rest of the flour in by hand. The dough will be very stiff. On a well-floured surface, roll out dough to a ½-inch thickness. Continually dust the rolling pin and board with flour. Press the springerle design into the dough surface with a springerle mold or pin. Press just firmly enough to make visible patterns on the dough. Cut cookies apart along pattern lines. Place individual cookie squares on an ungreased cookie sheet. Leave at room temperature for 10–12 hours.

Preheat oven to 300°. Before baking, dip a finger in cool water, rub the bottom of each cookie, and then return the cookie to the cookie sheet. Bake for 15 minutes. Store in tins at least 3 weeks to allow for aging.

One type of cookie the bakery sold all year was a small, round short-bread. A little dent was made in the top of the cookie, and when the cookie was cooled, a daub of frosting was placed in that dent. The icing would harden and form a wafer-like candy on the top. The cost of this sweet treat was two for a nickel. Elizabeth never bought those cookies and while in the bakery would often say, "Oh, we don't like those cookies!" Elizabeth's daughters, however, loved those cookies and would have a couple of nickels ready when they would walk home from school. Later, they would tease Elizabeth when she included a similar recipe, using preserve as the topping, in her cookbook, *We Make You Kindly Welcome*. To please her daughters, Elizabeth added a footnote that icing could be used instead.

"We Don't Like Those Cookies" Cookies

½ cup brown sugar
1 cup butter
2 egg yolks

½ teaspoon salt
1 teaspoon vanilla
2 cups all-purpose flour
¾ cup pecans, finely chopped

Cream brown sugar and butter until smooth. Mix in egg yolks, salt, and vanilla. Blend well. Stir in the flour until the batter is well blended. Cover bowl with a damp towel and chill for 1 hour.

Preheat oven to 350°. Grease the cookie sheet lightly. Roll dough into small balls about the size of a quarter. Gently coat each ball with chopped pecans. Place on a cookie sheet, gently press a finger on the top to form a dent, and slightly flatten each cookie. Bake for about 8–10 minutes, until slightly brown. When cooled, fill each dent with icing.

Icing for Cookies

1 cup confectioners' sugar
1–2 tablespoons boiling water
Drop of food coloring

Place sugar in a small mixing bowl. Gradually add boiling water while beating with an electric mixer at low speed. Add desired coloring, and beat until smooth and thick. Drop a small daub of icing into the dent, and let it stand until the icing becomes firm. When storing the cookies, place a sheet of waxed paper between layers to prevent cookies from sticking together.

Holidays continued to be a special time for the family. Country ham and roast turkey were part of the family's Christmas dinner tradition, one that included freshly made dressing balls, brown gravy, and twice-stuffed potatoes with grated sharp cheddar cheese.

Elizabeth was disappointed with Doc's inability to master the details of carving a turkey, which she considered to be a traditionally male role, even though she was better at the job herself. So they reached a compromise. Doc would carve a few slices, standing formally at the head of the table, and then the meat would be removed to the kitchen, where Elizabeth would make quick work of the carving and produce it on an ironstone platter. It took the children several years to realize how the holiday meal was really presented.

One Christmas, Elizabeth received a pressure cooker and was very happy to have this new, labor-saving piece of cookware. She used it for a variety of her favorite recipes. In a rush one day, Elizabeth decided to make split pea soup, but apparently, she didn't read the instructions thoroughly. The instructions included in large print: "The cooking of applesauce and dried peas is not recommended by the manufacturer." The pressure release valve blew off the pot and sent green pea soup to the kitchen ceiling, which was fifteen feet high. Doc came running to the kitchen when he heard Elizabeth scream in surprise. She used to tell her daughters that he reminded her what true love was when he told her to leave the kitchen and let him take care of the pressure cooker disaster.

Split Pea Soup

2 cups dried split peas
2 quarts water
½ teaspoon salt
1 cup diced celery
1 cup potatoes, diced

1 carrot, grated
1 medium onion, chopped
2 tablespoons flour
1 cup cream
Cream sherry to taste (optional)
Dash of red pepper
1 tablespoon minced celery leaves
½ cup cooked ham, diced*

Soak peas in 6–8 cups of cool water overnight. Drain and then cook peas in 2 quarts of water with salt, celery, potato, carrot, and onion. Simmer for 4–5 hours. Cool slightly and place in a blender in small portions. Blend until smooth and strain. Stir flour into cream and blend until smooth. Stir cream mixture into soup over low flame. Stir constantly as soup warms. When ready to serve, add sherry if desired. Sprinkle with a pinch of red pepper before serving. Garnish with celery leaves.

Two of Doc's favorite things were head cheese and pickled pig's feet. Although Elizabeth did not fix the head cheese from scratch, boiling the forehead, ears, feet, and scraps from a fresh pig, she did purchase it from the butcher and marinate it in vinegar. Then she used it as a cold cut for sandwiches and prepared a soup for Doc's lunch. However, Elizabeth did make her own pickled pig's feet and employed her daughters to wash and scrub them!

---

* For added flavor, if leftover ham is available, add to soup while reheating, or omit for a vegetarian version.

Pickled Pig's Feet

Wash fresh pig's feet and scrape them clean with a sturdy knife. Place them in a kettle with water to cover. Boil for 4–5 hours until soft. As they become slightly tender, add ¼-cup salt. Pack in a large jar or stone crock. Boil pickling spices and vinegar and pour this over the pig's feet. Let sit for 3–5 days. Slice them before serving.

Pem and Evalina were adolescents in the 1950s, and by the age of twelve, they had the freedom on Saturday mornings to take the Chestnut Street bus downtown to the movie theaters on Fourth Street in Louisville. If you got to the theater before noon, the cost of the ticket was reduced and, in those days, you could watch a movie continuously all day if desired.

Food was not allowed in the viewing area, so the girls would purchase an orange or grape drink and hot dogs from the Orange Bar. They would carry their treats in plain white bags and hide them as they entered the theater. The Rialto Theater on 616 South Fourth Street and the Loews (Palace Theater) at 625 South Fourth Street were beautiful to them, and they loved to sit on the balcony.

Many Saturday mornings, Elizabeth and Doc would go to the Haymarket off Jefferson Street in Old Louisville. The Haymarket was an outdoor farmer's market established in 1891. It occupied the block between Jefferson, Liberty, Floyd, and Brook Streets. Elizabeth would purchase whatever vegetables were in season from the market. The girls' favorite purchases were the artichokes. Doc used to say that artichokes were the one vegetable you'd have more pieces left over than when you had started eating them.

Artichokes

One artichoke per person
Boiling water for cooking
1 lemon, juiced
Melted butter
Lemon wedges for serving

Cut off the artichoke stems so that the vegetables will sit with the small end up on the bottom of a deep cooking pot. Add about 1½ inches of boiling water to the pot and add the lemon juice. Cover and simmer until one leaf on the outer edge pulls free easily, about 45–50 minutes. The age and size of the artichoke will determine the cooking time. Have a dish of melted butter ready for each person, place on a saucer with several lemon wedges on the side.

Mr. Blank had a farm in southern Indiana and would come across the river on Saturday mornings to sell at the Haymarket. Elizabeth would seek him out on these trips, and he would deliver the family fresh eggs and butter every two weeks and, in season, all sorts of delicious produce from his garden.

Being a homemaker did not stop Elizabeth from expanding her menus. The family became members of the Third Woodland Presbyterian Church at Thirty-Ninth and Broadway, and Elizabeth devoted much time to organizing church dinners and feeding youth groups.

She would often fall back on her favorite restaurant recipes, and as a result, many church members were able to enjoy fine restaurant meals like chicken à la king served with freshly made pastry shells, or croquettes made with cream mushroom gravy.

Grape and Mandarin Orange Salad

1 package lemon gelatin
¾ cup boiling water
1 cup cold water
1 can mandarin oranges, drained
1 cup seedless sliced grapes (red or green)

This may be made a day ahead. In a mixing bowl add gelatin to the hot water. Stir gently for 100 strokes; then add in cold water and stir 100 times again. Place oranges and grapes in an 8-by-8-inch glass dish. Add gelatin to the dish and swirl the mixture lightly with a fork to evenly distribute fruit. Place in the refrigerator to set. After gelatin has set, cover the dish with foil or plastic wrap to prevent drying out.

When ready to serve, place a square of gelatin on a leaf of lettuce, top with a daub of mayonnaise and add a sprig of parsley.

Tomato Aspic

2 cups cold tomato juice
1 envelope unflavored gelatin
1¼ cups hot tomato juice
⅛ teaspoon pepper
¼ teaspoon salt
1 tablespoon lemon juice
Dash of Tabasco

Place cold tomato juice in a mixing bowl and sprinkle gelatin on top. Gently stir until gelatin is dissolved. Stir in hot juice and blend well. Add the remaining ingredients. Pour into individual molds and chill until firm. Remove from molds and place on individual lettuce leaves. Dot with a daub of mayonnaise and place a parsley leaf on top.

Chicken à la King Pastry Shells

Preheat oven to 350°. Dough may be made from a basic piecrust recipe. Roll out dough to ¼-inch thickness and cut with a large biscuit cutter. Place each circle into the cup of a muffin pan and press lightly to the sides and bottom. Trim the top edges. Use tart shells if they are available. Bake shells for 8–10 minutes; then cool. Store in tins until ready to use. Do not stack the shells as they will be quite fragile. The shells may be made 2 days ahead and stored in tight tins.

Parker House Rolls

1 rounded cup of shortening
2 cups water, room temperature
1 cake dry yeast (2¼ teaspoons active dry yeast)
1 egg, beaten
6½ cups flour, divided
1 teaspoon salt
½ cup sugar
Melted butter

Melt shortening in a small saucepan and set aside to cool. Place the water in a large bowl and sprinkle yeast on top, stirring until dissolved. Add beaten egg and blend well. Divide half of the flour in a separate bowl. Stir salt and sugar into that flour. Stir this flour mixture into the yeast. When well mixed, add the remaining flour and knead into a ball. Cover with a damp towel. Set aside and let rise until doubled in size. Press down and place in the refrigerator in a covered container until the next day.

Preheat oven to 450°. When ready to bake, roll dough out on a floured surface to less than 2-inch thickness, and cut with a 1½-inch biscuit cutter. Brush with melted butter and fold over. Place in a tubular pan. Let rise until rolls look puffy. Bake for 10–15 minutes.

Peach Melba

1 cup raspberry jam
4 tablespoons water
1 loaf-shaped sponge cake
French vanilla ice cream
Canned peach halves
Whipped cream, unsweetened

In a saucepan, heat the jam and water to warm and blend until smooth; set aside. Place a 2-inch slice of cake in a shallow dessert dish. Cut a slice of ice cream to fit the size of the cake. Place a half peach slice on top of the ice cream, flat side down. Pour raspberry sauce over the top. Top with the whipped cream and a mint leaf.

Egg Kisses

4 egg whites
2 cups granulated sugar
2 teaspoons vanilla

Preheat oven to 250°. Place egg whites in a clean glass or metal mixing bowl and beat with an electric mixer until frothy. Continue beating and gradually add sugar. When the mixture becomes the consistency to stand in small peaks, add vanilla and blend well. Line a cookie sheet with parchment paper. Drop egg mixture by teaspoonfuls onto the paper to desired size (if to be used for fruit, make a small dent in the top with the back of a spoon). Bake for 20 minutes. Remove paper lining from the cookie sheet and let the kisses stand to cool and dry. Lift kisses off the paper gently with a thin, metal spatula. Store in tins until ready to use.

May be made a day ahead. The kisses can be made the size of a large marble to pop into your mouth or the size of a dessert cup and filled with fresh, cut-up fruit.

Egg Kisses and Fresh Peaches

Fresh peaches
Lemon juice
Granulated sugar
Unsweetened whipped cream

Wash and peel peaches; then cut them into slices. Toss with a small amount of lemon juice to prevent the peaches from browning. Gently stir in the sugar to desired sweetness. Leave in the refrigerator until ready to serve as the topping for egg kisses. Place a daub of unsweetened whipped cream on top and garnish with a mint leaf.

In 1950, the Kremer family moved to Northwestern Parkway, where the home overlooked the Shawnee Golf Course along the 10th fairway. The family had a view of the Indiana hills across the Ohio River. The sunsets were beautiful, and they often watched barges go up and down the river. When the Ohio would reach flood stage in spring and fall, the spotlights on the tugboats would shine on the back bedroom windows as beams searched the shores of the riverbanks to stay the course in the center of the river.

Pem's boyfriend during this time decided to build a canoe. When the Ohio spilled over its banks, the girls would spend hours paddling up and down their neighbor's backyards. It was great fun for the kids to launch the canoe from their very own backyard!

Their home was about two blocks from Fontaine Ferry, a sixty-four-acre amusement park in Western Louisville. On the Fourth of July, the family would have a picnic on their lower back porch and invite the girls' teenage friends. When it would get dark, the teens would head for the golf course with blankets to stretch out and watch the park's fireworks display.

In the winter months, the river would flood the golf course, and if the weather turned bitterly cold, the water would freeze. As the water receded, it sometimes left a two-inch coating of ice on the ground. Doc and some of the neighbors would put on ice skates or get sleds and metal garbage lids to play in the frozen waters.

Snowfalls brought friends from everywhere because the Kremers' steep, angled, terraced yards were perfect for sledding slopes that ended on the flat golf course. They had skis for adults and children, and Doc loved to ski over the grounds. He even put up a spotlight so that they wouldn't be limited by daylight hours. Everyone would come back home wet and cold through the garage, drop off their winter gear, and climb the basement steps to be greeted by a roaring fire. Elizabeth would have hot cocoa ready, along with hot buttered popcorn.

Hot Cocoa with Marshmallows

3 cups milk
6–7 tablespoons granulated sugar
1 cup boiling water

4 tablespoons cocoa
⅛ teaspoon salt
1 teaspoon vanilla

Scald milk over low heat. In another pan, combine sugar, water, cocoa, and salt in a double boiler. Place directly over low heat, stirring constantly, and bring to a boil. Continue stirring for 2 minutes. Add vanilla and blend well. Gradually add hot milk to the cocoa mixture and continue to heat, stirring constantly. Cover and remove from heat and let stand for 5 minutes. Beat with a hand mixer for 1 minute to prevent skin from forming on cocoa. Pour into large mugs. Place 2 large, fresh marshmallows on top. Serve immediately with a teaspoon for the melted marshmallow.

During Evalina and Pem's teenage years, a trip to the Iroquois Park Overlook meant Easter sunrise service for the church youth group. They would meet in the early morning hours at the Third Woodland Presbyterian Church at Thirty-Ninth and Broadway, where noisy adolescents and teenagers wearing blue jeans and warm coats would load into several cars. They would be dropped off at the base of the hill, where they would begin their vigorous climb up to the lookout. They would reach the top just in time for the amazing sunrise. The service was conducted by several Louisville churches, and the Kremer family held wonderful memories of this time. At the close of the service, everyone would head back down the hill and to the church, where breakfast was waiting. Elizabeth, along with other church women, would cook in the church basement while the children were making their climb.

Egg, Sausage, and Cheese Casserole

¼ cup butter, melted
¾ cup cheddar cheese, grated/diced
1 pound breakfast sausage, cooked
4 eggs
1 cup milk
Salt and pepper to taste
2 cups biscuit mix

Preheat oven to 350°. Grease an 8-by-8-inch baking dish. Arrange cheese on the bottom of the dish; sprinkle with cooked sausage. Beat eggs into the milk with a wire whisk until well blended. Season with salt and pepper. Stir biscuit mix into the egg mixture until smooth. Pour into the baking dish. Bake for 30 minutes or until set.

Bacon Buns

Breakfast bacon
1 package hot dog buns
Softened butter

Preheat oven to 350°. Fry bacon until crisp and set aside to drain on paper towels. Open buns and separate tops from buttons. Spread flat surface with butter and place on a cookie sheet. Toast in oven for about 5 minutes or until golden brown. Place strips of bacon on bun half and add the top. Arrange bacon buns in a basket containing a large thick napkin. Fold napkin over buns to keep warm.

The kitchen in the Kremer home on Northwestern Parkway was ten feet by six feet with twelve-foot ceilings. It was built around

1930 by a single man who lived in the house until the day he passed away. He had a cook the entire time he lived there. The kitchen had an apartment-size gas range, a double sink, and a built-in dishwasher on one side. The refrigerator had the motor on top and sat in an alcove on the narrow side of one wall. There were cabinets on the length and width of two walls, forming an L-shape. One of the cabinets was narrow but was the same height as the door and it held all of Elizabeth's spices. On the opposite wall from the sink were double swinging doors that led to the formal dining room. The other narrow wall had an outside entrance door and a window under which was a double-door, insulated milk delivery box. There was only a small, drop-leaf, metal utility table for food preparation. The kitchen was tiny. As a result, it consistently amazed the family how Elizabeth could prepare extravagant meals in such a small space. One of the girls' friends said that she could never remember Elizabeth actually being in the kitchen and only recalled her magically appearing with a beautiful display of food.

On the other side of the dining room was a door off in the corner that led up to the attic. The first few steps curved up, and Elizabeth used this as a pantry because it stayed cool.

Breakfast was a treat in the Kremer house, but on special breakfast days, Elizabeth would make a morning meal of a fried egg over a broiled T-bone steak. For lunch, there were basic sandwich rules that were passed down to the children. The crust was always to be cut from the bread. The bread slices should be covered in a thin coating of mayonnaise or butter, depending on the type of sandwich filling. Sandwiches were to be sliced on the diagonal because the diamond shape is nicer to handle when eating. Packed school lunches for Pem and Evalina were generally shrimp salad, cucumber, ham salad, or egg salad sandwiches.

Egg Salad Sandwiches

4 eggs
1 tablespoon sweet pickle relish
Salt and pepper to taste
Mayonnaise

Boil eggs to the hard-boiled stage, rinse in cold water, then crack, peel, and let cool. Cut the eggs into small pieces and place in a mixing bowl. Work lightly with a fork. Add relish and seasoning and continue to mix gently with a fork. Gradually add enough mayonnaise to desired thickness of spread. Let the egg salad rest in the refrigerator for 1 hour before making sandwiches. Spread one bread slice with the egg salad, and place a fresh leaf of lettuce on top. Place the remaining bread slice on top, and cut on the diagonal.

Elizabeth's peanut butter sandwiches were a special treat for the girls' lunch at school. She would spread softened butter on each slice of bread, then a thin layer of peanut butter on each slice, and finally jelly. Following the sandwich rules, crusts were removed, and the sandwiches were cut on the diagonal.

Shrimp Salad Sandwiches

Large wedge of lemon
2 cups shrimp, peeled and cut into small pieces
Salt and pepper to taste
2 tablespoons finely chopped celery
Enough mayonnaise to make spreadable

Squeeze lemon over the shrimp in a small mixing bowl and toss gently. Season with salt and pepper. Stir in celery and blend, gradually adding mayonnaise to desired consistency. Spread on sandwich bread and add a leaf of lettuce.

For lunch, the shrimp salad was often made with leftover shrimp from the night before. For a larger group, Elizabeth would buy the pullman loaf from the bakery. A pullman loaf is made in a special pan that helps keep its square shape. As an oversized loaf, it was good for sandwiches, and the square shape made for easy and even crust removal. Lunch on Saturdays was equally wonderful for the family, and Welsh rarebit was one of the family's favorites.

Welsh Rarebit

3¼ cups cheddar cheese
3 tablespoons water
¾ cup lukewarm milk
2 teaspoons Worcestershire sauce
2 teaspoons dry mustard
¼ teaspoon salt
Dash of pepper
Paprika

Cut cheese into small cubes and place in the top of a double boiler with the water. Stir constantly to melt the cheese. When it's smooth, gradually add the milk in small amounts to prevent the cheese from cooling. When well blended, add all seasonings but paprika. Serve on a luncheon platter over freshly toasted bread slices. Sprinkle the tops with a bit of paprika.

One of the girls' friends, Sandy, once told them that she loved coming to the Kremer house because even though Doc and Elizabeth were older, they were very laid back. She thought they were very "academic," and Elizabeth let Sandy borrow her copy of *Auntie Mame*, which was the first book that Evalina read for pleasure. Sandy also remembered one day when Doc let the girls drive his car out to the first major mall that opened in Louisville. There were live lobsters for sale at the mall, and the girls pooled all their money to buy one. They recalled it made noises in the paper sack all the way home, and they named him Oscar. When they got to the Kremer house, Elizabeth prepared the live lobster for dinner. Sandy recalled that it was the first time she had ever experienced this kind of cooking and that it was the only time she had ever eaten lobster, even after she became an adult. Perhaps, it was the memory of Oscar trying to escape the boiling pot!

There were so many recipes that the family enjoyed during this time. Memories of family meals were mixed with the sound of Doc playing and singing at the piano and the smell of his fat cigar hanging out the side of his mouth.

Pear and Roquefort Cheese Salad

Bibb or Boston lettuce
½ canned pear per person
Roquefort cheese, cut into desired-size cubes
Cheddar cheese, grated

Lay washed lettuce on a small salad dish. Place the pear with the round side down. Place a cube of cheese in the pear indentation. Garnish with a small amount of grated cheddar. Serve with Anna's French dressing.

Anna's French Dressing

6 tablespoons oil
Squeeze of lemon juice
2 tablespoons vinegar (more if using olive oil)
1 teaspoon sugar
Salt to taste (at least ¼ teaspoon)
Paprika (at least ¼ teaspoon)
One sliver of onion

Put all the ingredients in a bottle. Shake well and refrigerate.

Grapefruit and Avocado Salad

1 grapefruit
1 avocado
Lettuce leaves
Salt and pepper to taste

Peel and cut grapefruit and avocado into thin slices. Place on lettuce leaves. Sprinkle with salt and fresh ground pepper. Place Anna's French dressing in a decorative container on the table.

Breaded Pork Chops

4 thick pork chops
1 egg, beaten
3 tablespoons milk
Salt and pepper
Fine bread crumbs
4 tablespoons shortening

Score the fat on the edge of the chops to keep the pork from curling. Whip egg and milk together with a wire whisk. On a piece of waxed paper, place the bread crumbs and sprinkle with desired amount of seasoning; mix lightly by hand. Dip the chops on both sides into the egg mixture and then press into the bread-crumb mixture on both sides. Place the chops on a platter and allow to dry for 10–15 minutes. In a heavy skillet, melt shortening over low heat. Cook slowly to ensure the meat is thoroughly cooked in the center. Fry slowly on each side till it's golden brown.

Spaghetti Italian

2 pounds ground chuck
1 cup onions, chopped
1 (28 ounce) can tomatoes, crushed
1 tablespoon oregano
1 teaspoon salt
2 tablespoons butter
1 (8 ounce) can tomato sauce
6 mushrooms, sliced
2 teaspoons basil
¼ teaspoon pepper
Parmesan cheese, grated

Brown meat in a large, heavy skillet. Add onions and cook for 10 minutes. Drain off the fat. Add all remaining ingredients but the Parmesan cheese, and continue cooking over low heat for 2 hours, stirring occasionally to prevent sticking. Serve over cooked spaghetti, and top with grated Parmesan cheese.

Pan-Fried Oysters

Standard oysters
Salt
Pepper

2 tablespoons water
Egg yolk
Fine bread crumbs
Oil

Drain oysters and pour cold water over them. Lay out on a cloth to dry and pat the tops lightly. Place on waxed paper and sprinkle with salt and pepper. In a small bowl, whisk water and egg yolks. Dip oysters in the egg mixture and then bread crumbs. Let stand for 5 minutes and repeat. Place on a flat surface and allow to dry for 10–15 minutes. Heat oil in a heavy skillet over low heat and fry oysters to a light brown. Serve with cocktail sauce.

Quick Cocktail Sauce

2 teaspoons prepared horseradish
1 cup ketchup
2 drops hot sauce

Place ingredients in a small bowl and blend until smooth.

Floating Island Prune Whip

1 cup stewed prunes, pitted
Pinch of salt
1 egg white
2 level tablespoons granulated sugar
Homemade custard

Stew prunes according to the package directions. Rub prunes through a strainer. Mix the salt, egg white, and sugar with a hand mixer at high speed until frothy; add prunes and continue beating until the mixture will hold peaks. Chill in the refrigerator. When ready to serve, scoop the prune whip into individual dessert dishes that contain about ½ cup of homemade custard.

Custard for Prune Whip

1 tablespoon all-purpose flour
2 cups milk, divided
3 egg yolks
½ cup granulated sugar
1 teaspoon vanilla

Stir flour into one cup of milk until smooth and set aside. Heat remaining milk in a saucepan over low heat until a film is present on the surface of the scalded milk. Remove the skim and add flour mixture, stirring with a whisk continuously. In the top pan of a double boiler, beat the egg yolks and sugar together. Add a small portion of hot milk to the egg mixture, stir constantly (this must be done slowly to prevent curdling). Keep adding milk to the egg mixture until fully incorporated. Place blended mixtures over boiling water. Continue cooking until the mixture is thickened or until it coats a metal spoon. Stir in the vanilla. Let cool, and then store in a jar in the refrigerator.

Pumpkin Pie

1½ cups canned pumpkin
¾ cups granulated sugar
½ teaspoon salt
1 teaspoon cinnamon
¼ teaspoon ginger
¼ teaspoon cloves
¼ teaspoon nutmeg
3 eggs, slightly beaten
1¼ cups milk
1 (6 ounce) can evaporated milk
1 unbaked pie shell
Unsweetened whipped cream

Preheat oven to 400°. Blend pumpkin, sugar, salt, and spices well. Slowly add eggs and milk, and then blend well with a mixer. Pour filling into the shell. Bake for 50 minutes. Pie is done when a knife inserted in the middle comes away clean. Let cool before serving, and top with unsweetened whipped cream.

Crunchy Peanut Butter Cookies

1 cup flour
½ teaspoon baking soda
½ teaspoon salt
⅓ cup plus 1 tablespoon brown sugar, firmly packed
½ cup granulated sugar
½ cup crunchy peanut butter
½ cup butter
1 egg, beaten slightly
¾ teaspoon vanilla

Preheat oven to 350°. Sift dry flour, soda, and salt together and set aside. Cream sugars, peanut butter, and butter until smooth. Stir in egg and mix well. Add vanilla. Begin adding flour slowly and blend well. The batter will be stiff. Drop by teaspoonfuls onto a lightly greased cookie sheet. Press the top of the dropped cookie twice with a sugared fork, making a crossed print. Bake for 10–12 minutes. Cool on racks and store in tins.

Refrigerator Cookies

1 cup soft butter
1 teaspoon vanilla
1 cup powdered sugar
2½ cups flour
¼ teaspoon salt

Cream butter, vanilla, and sugar until smooth. Mix in flour and salt by hand. Form into a 2-inch roll and wrap in wax paper. Place in the refrigerator overnight.

Preheat oven to 350°. Cut dough in ⅛-inch slices and place on a lightly greased cookie sheet. Sprinkle the cookies with sugar. Bake until the edges become a light golden brown, about 10–12 minutes. Cool on racks and store in tins.

Caramel Sauce for Ice Cream

2 cups brown sugar
¾ cup cream
½ cup butter
1 teaspoon vanilla

Boil sugar, cream, and butter. Transfer to a mixing bowl and beat until creamy. Add vanilla and beat until smooth. Caramel sauce is delicious as a topping for ice cream or cake.

Elizabeth felt strongly that basic table manners were critical, and for years, she taught and encouraged her daughters to have proper dining etiquette. Instructions on proper table manners began at an early age for Pem and Evalina, and eventually they became second nature to the girls. To lean on one's elbows on the table was gently corrected by "You mustn't put your elbows on the table" or by a joking reminder: "Evalina, Pem, strong and able, take your elbows off the table."

A slight touch to the middle of the spine as she placed food on the table was a signal to sit up straight. Other times, there was a familiar "Hold your head high" or "Don't lean on the back of your chair." At a very young age, Evalina and Pem were taught the following rules of table etiquette:

> To hold the knife and fork correctly
> To eat without the slightest sound from the lips
> To drink a beverage quietly
> To make no noise with any implement at the table
> To eat slowly and chew the food thoroughly
> To not slurp one's soup
> To observe others at the table and wait for the hostess to begin eating

These skills instilled confidence in the girls and carried them into adulthood. Elizabeth had a unique way of giving a look or simply setting her lips, a gesture that made the girls instantly know to take inventory of their actions and correct a situation immediately. It must have had the same effect on her servers, who snapped to attention whenever Elizabeth appeared. Even her grandchildren were affected; they referred to the "grandmother look."

Evalina and Pem learned early the proper use of table serving pieces and flatware. When confronted with multiple silverware, start at the outside to the far left and right and work your way in toward the plate. When in doubt, watch the hostess, as knowing which piece to use was part of her job.

Knife should be held toward the end of the handle with the forefinger being the only finger to touch the blade and that only along the backside of the blade at the root, no further down toward the top of the blade.

Fork: when cutting food with a knife and a fork, the fork should be turned over and used to steady the food as the knife is drawn slowly over to cut the food into small pieces. Lay the knife noiselessly and diagonally across the upper part of the plate.

Switch the fork to the other hand, turn it over, and place the food in the mouth with the fork level with the mouth. The fork should be cradled in the hand with the patterned side up. Be sure to hold the fork near the end of the handle. When the fork is not in use, it should be left on the plate parallel to the edge of the table. Most entrées are eaten with a fork, but it is acceptable to eat soupy vegetables with a spoon.

Spoon: never leave in a cup or glasses. Soup spoons are provided for liquid dishes and should be left on the rim of the soup platter that is placed under the bowl.

Multiple forks and spoons that are part of the table setting: start using the utensils from the farthest one out and work inward toward the plate.

The napkin is usually folded and placed to the left of the plate; the napkin should be unfolded and placed on the lap, never tucked at the neck of the shirt.

If a napkin ring is on the napkin, the ring should be removed and placed at the upper left of the plate. When the meal is completed, the napkin should be reinserted into the ring.

Upon completion of the meal, place the knife and fork across the plate to keep them from slipping off the plate when being removed.

The bread plate is placed on the left side of the dinner plate and above the fork. The butter knife may be placed above the plate or to the right side of the bread plate.

When eating bread, rolls, or biscuits, they should be broken into manageable pieces. These pieces should be held in the hand and buttered with the tip of the butter knife.

Drink a beverage by bringing the glass perpendicular to the lips, and lift at a slight angle. Drink slowly, and do not pour the beverage down your throat with loud gulps. Take a swallow and pause. If sweetening iced tea, do not stir with such violent movements as to clink the spoon against the side of the glass and make a disturbing noise.

With Elizabeth's restaurant skills, she felt some of her knowledge should be part of her children's basic upbringing. They regularly had napkin and finger bowl practice, according to the following rules:

Finger bowls should be placed on paper doilies on a saucer and set on a sideboard or side table in the dining area. Fill bowls half full with water. A thin slice of lemon should be placed in the water. After the main course, bowls should be placed in front of the guest from their left serving side. Fingertips should be dipped in the water, lemon may be gently squeezed over fingers, rubbing fingertips together will help remove oil from fingers. Pat fingers dry with the napkin.

All the seasons held opportunities for special meals and cooking. In the winter, being snowed in meant family adventures in cooking. Evalina's birthday was in February, and quite often the family could not go out to celebrate because of challenging road conditions. One snowbound birthday, Evalina decided to make her own angel food cake from scratch, with Elizabeth's guidance, of course. Evalina was just learning how to cook, and she labored all day, sifting the flour and beating the egg whites until at last her cake was finished. They left the cake to cool and dry on a side counter in the kitchen and went to the living room to play canasta in front of the fireplace. After a while, they went back into the kitchen for hot chocolate and popcorn only to find Tink, their cat, up on the counter eating the precious angel food cake. Tink had started in the center and had worked his way all the way out toward the sides. The cat was sick for two days, and Evalina was disgusted. After that incident, she switched to chocolate meringue pie as her birthday choice for dessert.

Chocolate Meringue Pie

1 package of Royal Chocolate Pudding
1 cooked pie shell
Thick meringue

Make the pudding according to packing directions. Cook the piecrust accordingly as well. Pour the pudding into the crust and let cool while preparing the meringue.

Meringue

½ teaspoon cream of tartar
3 egg whites
6 tablespoons granulated sugar
½ teaspoon vanilla

Preheat oven to 400°. Place cream of tartar in egg whites and beat until frothy. Gradually beat in sugar. Continue beating until peaks begin to form. Quickly beat in vanilla. Spoon meringue on pie filling, covering the entire area with the back of a spoon, forming peaks. Be sure to spread up to the piecrust to seal the edges; this will keep the meringue from shrinking away from the crust during baking. Bake pie for 8 minutes. Cool completely before serving.

Fudge Pie

2 squares chocolate (2 ounces)
½ cup butter
1 cup sugar
2 eggs, separated
½ cup flour, sifted
1 teaspoon vanilla

Preheat oven to 325°. Melt chocolate in a double boiler and let cool. Beat butter until soft and blend in sugar, creaming well. Beat in egg yolks. Next blend in melted chocolate; add flour and vanilla. Stir well. Egg whites should be beaten until stiff and folded into chocolate mixture. Pour into a greased 8-inch pie pan and bake for 30 minutes. Serve pie topped with vanilla ice cream.

Elizabeth's desserts were many and wonderful. She had a collection of cookbooks that went everywhere with her as she moved around. She had everything from old, classic cookbooks to small corporate promotional booklets. One such booklet was published by Walter Baker & Company, 1908, the first company to produce chocolate in the United States. It had wonderful recipes for chocolate but also included the following statement to justify its use: "The people who make constant use of chocolate are the ones who enjoy the most steady health, and are the least subject to a multitude of little ailments which destroy the comfort of life; their plumpness is also equal. These are two advantages which everyone may verify among his own friends, wherever the practice is used." The booklet was titled, *Choice Recipes*, by Miss Maria Parloa and other noted teachers.

Someone had to keep the kitchen implements in good working condition and Doc was the knife-sharpening expert of the family. As a result, Elizabeth always had well-honed knives. The whetstone was passed down through the family as well as the knowledge of taking one's time to spread the fingers just so and applying the right pressure on the upper part of the blade. In gentle gliding motions, the whetstone is stroked the same number of times on each side to get the best edge. Doc instructed the girls that they must dampen the stone with a small amount of oil or water. Elizabeth taught Evalina and Pem how to cut up a chicken with those same expertly sharpened knives.

How to Cut Up Chicken

Place the fowl on a cutting board. Use a sharp knife and cut through the skin on the inside of the legs next to the body. Slash the skin and meat to the joint. With both hands, snap the joint. Place a knife at the joint and cut through the meat and skin. Pull the wings out from the body and slash skin to joint, snap joint and finish cutting through to separate wings from body. Starting at the wing socket, insert the knife and cut the rib bones along the back to the tail of the chicken. Spread back from the breast and snap base of the wishbone. Pull apart breasts from back. To split the breastbone, hold the chicken with the rib cage upward. Lay the knife on the breastbone and strike the knife with a mallet. This will lay apart the breast. Use the knife to cut through the skin and meat. When this is complete, it will yield the backbone, gizzard, and liver for soup broth; two wings; two legs; and two breasts to fry, broil, or bake.

Even meals after holidays were wonderful, and these different and delightful mealtimes were called "get-away days" by Elizabeth. This was when she would use up all the leftovers from holiday meals. It was not only a way to save money and reduce food waste but also a way for Elizabeth to continue her creativity in the kitchen.

Vegetable Soup

Leftover pot roast meat and bone
2 quarts water
2 carrots, sliced
2 stalks celery, sliced
¼ teaspoon ground cloves
Salt and pepper
½ onion, chopped
1 can tomato sauce

In a large soup pot, place leftover meat and bone. Add water, carrots, celery, seasoning, onion, and tomato sauce. Cook for 1 hour.

Ham Salad

Grind leftover baked ham pieces and place in a mixing bowl. Add a small amount of sweet pickle relish and stir in lightly. Blend in ¼ teaspoon of Dijon mustard and enough mayonnaise to make a smooth spread. Store in the refrigerator until ready to use. Smooth a thin coat of mayo on bread (cut crust off first), and then spread ham salad. Add a piece of leaf lettuce and slice the sandwich on the diagonal.

Ham and Scalloped Potatoes

Potatoes, sliced
Onion, chopped, divided
Ham chunk or slices
Salt and pepper
Hot milk

Preheat oven to 375°. Peel desired amount of potato and slice ¼ inch thick. Place a layer of potatoes on the bottom of a 9-by-12-inch buttered baking dish. Sprinkle a layer with half of the onions, ham, salt, and pepper. Repeat layer using remaining onion. Heat milk to hot but not boiling. Pour over potatoes and cover with foil. Bake for 1½ hours. Remove foil for the last 15–20 minutes. Let cook for 10 minutes and serve.

Pot Pies

2 cups water
2 cubes chicken bouillon
1 celery rib, sliced
½ cup onion, chopped
2 carrots, diced
1 small potato, diced
½ cup peas
Salt and pepper
2–3 cups shredded turkey or chicken
2 tablespoons flour
Biscuit dough

Preheat oven to 350°. In a large pot, heat water and dissolve bouillon in it. Add celery, onion, carrots, and potatoes. Cook until tender, strain, and reserve liquid. Pour liquid back into pot and add peas, salt, and pepper. Keep warm over medium heat. Place meat and vegetables in individual baking dishes and set aside. In a cup, make a flour paste with 1–2 tablespoons of the bouillon. Add paste to the pot, stirring constantly to thicken. Pour over the meat and vegetables, leaving room to place a thin biscuit dough on the top of each dish. Bake until the crust is cooked in the center and a golden brown.

Hash

1 cup cooked potatoes
½ cup onion, chopped
¼ cup celery, chopped
1 tablespoon butter
1 or more cups of leftover gravy
2 cups leftover chicken or turkey[†]
Salt and pepper to taste

Peel and dice potatoes, cover with water, and boil until tender. Drain. In a small saucepan, sauté the onion and celery in the butter until tender. Combine the gravy, meat, celery mixture, and potatoes in a large pot. Heat until hot. Serve with corn bread. To increase the amount of gravy, dissolve chicken or beef bouillon in a cup of boiling water and add to gravy. Thicken with flour paste.

Marinated Asparagus

½ cup sugar
2 tablespoons water
¼ teaspoon ground cinnamon
¼ cup apple cider vinegar
4 whole cloves
½ teaspoon salt
½ teaspoon celery seed
Cooked asparagus

Heat ingredients and pour over leftover cooked asparagus. Place in a closed container in the refrigerator for at least 3 hours. Serve as a side to luncheon sandwiches.

[†] If using beef instead, add 1 teaspoon Worcestershire sauce to gravy.

Stewed Fried Corn

Corn, cut from the cob
2 tablespoons butter
3 tablespoons flour
2 tablespoons sugar
Salt and pepper to taste
¾ cup milk

Cut kernels from leftover cooked corn cobs. In a heavy skillet over medium heat, melt butter and stir in corn, flour, sugar, and seasoning. Continue stirring until bubbly. Slowly add milk. Heat, stirring constantly, until mixture is hot and thickened. Remove from heat and serve.

Deviled Eggs

Peel leftover Easter eggs, or hard-boil eggs and then peel. Rinse in cold water and cut into half. Gently separate the yolks from the whites. Place the whites on a platter. With a fork, crumble yolks in a small mixing bowl. Add a small amount of apple cider vinegar to taste. Stir in salt and pepper to taste. Add a small amount of mayonnaise to desired consistency. Gently spoon yolk mixture into the center of the egg white, place a single parsley leaf on each egg half, and sprinkle with paprika.

Basic White Sauce

2 tablespoons butter
2 tablespoons flour
Salt and pepper to taste
1 cup milk

Melt butter, stir in flour and seasoning. Cook over low heat until smooth and bubbly. Slowly stir in milk. Continue cooking and stirring until the sauce has reached desired thickness.

Creamed Eggs on Baked Potatoes or Toast

Preheat oven to 350°. Wash desired number of potatoes. Prick with a fork and grease with butter. Cover potatoes with foil and bake until tender. Peel leftover Easter eggs and rinse or hard boil eggs and then peel. Slice with an egg slicer and have the slices ready to fold into hot white sauce at the last minute. When everything is ready, place an unwrapped potato on the center of a breakfast plate. Cut a cross in the top of the potato and gently press down while squeezing with thumb and index fingers; this will open the potato. Gently fold the sliced egg into the hot white sauce, and scoop in the center of the slit potato, allowing the sauce to run over the side of the skin. Sprinkle it with a dash of paprika.

Pie Crust Cuttings with Cinnamon Sugar

After making crusts for pie, place the trimmings on a small cookie sheet and sprinkle with a mixture of cinnamon sugar. Place in the oven beside the pie. Cook strips for 5–8 minutes. Remove from the oven and cool on a small saucer. Serve to waiting children (or adults).

Elizabeth was known to make most meals using only basic ingredients, with nothing premade. There came to be two premade exceptions that she was loyal to: Hellmann's mayonnaise (my apologies to the Duke's mayonnaise purists) and Duncan Hines cake mix. Instant cake mixes were a controversial subject for traditionalists, who insisted that good cakes must be made from scratch, but Elizabeth was not an old-fashioned cook. After she tried several brands and decided that Duncan Hines was the best, she rarely made a cake from scratch again. She did, however, balance out this convenience with a traditional cooked frosting from the Victorian era.

Elizabeth's Instant Angel Food Cake

Prepare cake mix according to package instructions. Pour batter into tube pan, bake, and then place over a small soda bottle to hold inverted cake in pan while cooling and drying.

Cooked Mint Frosting

5 tablespoons cold water
2 unbeaten egg whites
1½ cups sugar
¼ teaspoon cream of tartar
2–3 drops essence of peppermint
1 drop green food coloring

Place water in the bottom pan of a double boiler and bring to a rapid boil. Put egg whites, sugar, and cream of tartar in the top boiler, and mix at low speed until combined. Place over boiling water, and beat the ingredients on high speed for approximately 7 minutes. Frosting is ready when it stands in peaks. Remove the top pan from heat and add two drops of peppermint. Add a tiny drop of food coloring and beat in quickly; too much beating will cause it to turn into sugar. The frosting should just have a slight tint of green. Spread frosting on cake with the back of a serving spoon, spreading gently to create small peaks around the side and top of cake. Decorate with a few mint leaves around base of cake and a small bunch of long mint stems to place in center of cake.

Elizabeth would often let her daughters help with baking the cake and, when they were older, with the frosting. Even still, Elizabeth added the mint essence herself to get just the right flavor and added the food coloring until the color met her approval. This cake, a blend of old and new, was often used as a centerpiece on the dining table, but sometimes it was served theatrically and presented at the last moment with a flourish. Elizabeth's recipe also noted that one should always have fresh mint growing somewhere nearby!

Despite the wonderful memories and good family times, around 1950, Elizabeth and Doc began to have a few problems. Like so many of that era, the evening cocktail was an entrenched part of their lifestyle. It helped to relax them at the end of the day, but those drinks had become more frequent and felt more like a necessity. As a result, family arguments happened more frequently, especially when these two strong-willed individuals with differing opinions came up against each other. For a while during this time, the arguments became a nightly occurrence.

So, by the mid-'50s, Elizabeth decided that drinking was no longer soothing her nerves and was out of hand. She joined Alcoholics Anonymous, and within a year, Doc joined her. Together they began a new stage of their lives and put drinking behind them. Putting the past aside, they moved forward with newfound friends.

Doc loved to travel, and Elizabeth loved to travel with him. He never went to the same place the same way twice. When

Evalina and Pem grew up and moved away, he would find new routes for his trips in order to visit them from Louisville, Kentucky, even if that meant traveling through Charleston, South Carolina, on the way to New Orleans, Louisiana. With their children grown, the Kremers enjoyed their lives, their travels together, their shared meals, church life, and family.

Sadly, in August 1966, Doc became ill, and on November 13, he passed away from cancer. Upon his request, he was cremated, and his ashes were scattered in the Ohio River, a fitting place that was filled with many joyous memories. Before he passed away but near the end, Doc was mostly unresponsive. Nonetheless, Elizabeth stayed by his side. She was so dedicated that Evalina and Pem had to convince their mother to take the time to even eat. One of those times, as Elizabeth gathered her coat and was placing her hat on her head, Doc opened his eyes and looked right at Elizabeth. In a youthful voice, much like during their courting days, and a twinkle in his eyes, he asked, "Where're you going, kid?" Little did they all know that Elizabeth was going to Shakertown at Pleasant Hill.

5

Shaker Your Plate

There were a total of nineteen Shaker villages, including two in Kentucky: Pleasant Hill, established in 1805; and South Union, in 1807. The Shakers were a religious group whose tenets included simplicity, celibacy, and work. They lived communally and shared all their property. They were a practical but self-sufficient and innovative group. The Shakers at Pleasant Hill built a series of buildings with precision and permanence in mind. For a time, they were a quite successful community, specializing in handmade brooms, animals, garden seeds, preservation, vegetables, and the breeding of prized cattle. Their growth relied on conversion and missionary work, which is how the Pleasant Hill settlement began. Growth was difficult, and as a celibate society, this took its toll. Pleasant Hill was dissolved in 1910, and the last Shaker died in 1923. Small efforts were made over the years to rehabilitate the property, but it wasn't until 1960 that a small group formed to revive interest in Shakertown, as the Pleasant Hill group was known. In 1961, it created a new, nonprofit educational corporation known as Shakertown at Pleasant Hill Kentucky, Inc. The corporation was to acquire, restore, and interpret the nineteenth-century village as a living museum, with a goal to create an educational and cultural center in the area.

James L. Cogar, who had been the curator at Colonial Williamsburg, returned to his native state and took on the task of overseeing the restoration of the village. Earl D. Wallace had retired in 1965 as an associate of the Wall Street investment banking firm of Dillon, Read, and Company, where he oversaw private investments in oil and gas properties. As a Kentucky native and graduate of the University of Kentucky, Wallace became interested in the restoration. Joining with the corporation, he began to raise funds to set the wheels in motion for the restoration of the village. Wallace laughingly stated, "I raised the money, and Jim spent it." At the time, Wallace approached Elizabeth to see if she would be interested in operating a restaurant in Shakertown, but she turned down the offer. He looked for and contacted others but didn't have anyone lined up for the position.

With Doc's passing, December 1966 was a very hard month for Elizabeth, but in January 1967, Earl Wallace and his secretary, Betty Walsh Morris (who happened to be Elizabeth's niece, the daughter of her sister Belle) paid her a visit. Robert "Bob" Jewell, son of Asa and Lizzie Jewell, was one of the Shakertown trustees, and he encouraged Wallace to ask Elizabeth if she would reconsider. Earl and Betty asked Elizabeth to come to Mercer County, Kentucky, to oversee and manage a restaurant in the newly restored Shaker Village at Pleasant Hill.

The Kremer family was familiar with Shakertown. During the 1940s and 1950s, Doc would drive from Louisville to Harrodsburg via US Route 68 to reach Jessamine County, Kentucky, where Elizabeth owned a forty-nine-acre farm. Despite the conventions of the time, Doc had encouraged Elizabeth to invest her profits from the Canary Cottage in land. Not only did Elizabeth purchase the land in 1937, but Doc also recommended that the property be in her name only—yet another example of how Elizabeth and Doc broke social norms and practiced an unconventional equality between the sexes.

When the family would make the drive to Jessamine County, they would pass by the then boarded-up village of Pleasant

Hill. As they would drive by, Doc would slow down and announce "This is the Shakertown." The girls thought the village was spooky and scary because most of the buildings were covered in ivy, some were falling down, and others were completely boarded up. This was before interest had grown in American heritage and historic preservation.

So while Shakertown was familiar to Elizabeth, this job offer was a huge decision. She was a new widow, and coming out of retirement at sixty-five years of age to launch a new career was frightening. Elizabeth had been out of the business for twenty-seven years, and she worried that she wouldn't be as capable as she was earlier. With the encouragement of her daughters, who assured her that the worst thing that could happen was falling flat on her face, she forged ahead. With the support and even nagging of Pem and Evalina, Elizabeth agreed to open a small sandwich shop in the Old Stone Shop.

Pleasant Hill started with twenty buildings on 110 acres that lay on both sides of US 68 in Mercer County, Kentucky. The Old Stone Shop, built in 1811, was once the home and office of Dr. Pennebaker, the Shaker doctor. Over time, it had been used for a variety of purposes. During this time, the stone shop had become the temporary home of James C. Thomas, an assistant hired by Jim Cogar as work began on the buildings. By 1968, Thomas was in charge of the hostesses in the exhibit buildings, the furniture crew, and the gift shop.

The Old Stone Shop was built using large-cut limestone. There were eight steps leading up from the old road through the village. A bypass had been built, and the old road was closed, which meant guest parking was no problem. The Old Stone Shop had three floors and sat on the east side of the village. It had two large rooms on the main floor and a small kitchen in an enclosed area of the back porch. A screened-in porch went across the back

The Old Stone Shop at Shaker Village. UKL, Clay Lancaster Kentucky Architectural Photographs, 2014av001.

to the side of the kitchen, and this became the summer kitchen used to feed the staff, the trustees, local residents, and tourists. It was a soup, salad, and dessert place that served simple fare in a grand style.

The downstairs was set up with a service counter in the right front room, where lunch orders were placed. The customers would then take a table either in the left dining room or pass through that area to the screened-in back porch. The porch was the favorite location for guests.

By the summer of 1967, the Old Stone Shop was ready to open to the public. All the health department regulations were met, and the restaurant was to be opened with Elizabeth Cromwell Kremer at the helm. Not just all of Elizabeth's family and friends but also the Shakertown trustees felt that opening this small restaurant would give Elizabeth a chance to ease back into the business.

The upstairs of the Old Stone Shop was divided into two rooms, one larger and the other smaller, along with one restroom. The Old Stone Shop became home to Elizabeth and Mildred Elliott. Mildred was from Campbellsville, Kentucky, and had been married to Margaret Elliott Jewell's brother, Milton Elliott. Like Elizabeth, she was a widow and had been persuaded by Bob Jewell to both keep Elizabeth company for the summer and work in the restaurant. Mildred had tons of energy and, unlike Elizabeth, drove and had her own car. The two widows moved a few belongings to the second floor of the Old Stone Shop and began their Shaker summer adventure.

When the restaurant opened, the menu was sparse. There was a basic soup, a salad, sandwich, and dessert. They soon hired cooks, and the Shaker restaurant business began in earnest. The counter where orders were placed was a solid piece of wood at a height of around forty inches. Elizabeth had not been consulted on the counter's construction, and surely if she had, there wouldn't have been an issue. But as a result, she and Mildred didn't have direct access to the customers without having to go through the kitchen to the back porch and then come back around to where the guest tables were. It was inefficient to have one person on each side of the counter and made for bad customer service.

Of course, the workmen were busy with restoration projects in the village and although they never missed their employee meals, cutting the counter to allow for a lift section was not a priority over the building work. One day, however, when the project heads came in for lunch, Mildred, who was in her late sixties, hoisted herself backward onto the counter, flipped her legs over it to the front, and hopped down to deliver the meals. The group was so surprised that all they could do was stare. Needless to say, the flip counter was cut the very next day! News traveled fast about the delicious food, and soon this very small restaurant was packed with local workmen, architects, and travelers.

The road leading out of Pleasant Hill was blocked by a huge heavy chain and a padlock. Mildred and Elizabeth wanted a key so that they could go out during the evenings. They talked their way into getting a duplicate key, but to get Mildred's car out at night, the two had to work together. One would straddle the chain and lift it so the other could get the lock opened and then unwrap the chain from the post located on one side of the road. Mildred would drive the car over the chain, and then the two of them would work together to get it securely back in place. This procedure was repeated on the return trip, and it took ten minutes each time. But this allowed the two women to have freedom to explore and enjoy their time off work.

Mildred and Elizabeth made a good team, balancing a shared adventurous spirit, great humor, years of shared experience, and a thorough knowledge of Kentucky food and hospitality. With their freedom and Mildred's car, the two went on weekly adventures to discover Kentucky's food excellence. One such quest was to find the best in Kentucky country hams; they picked Taylor's in Cynthiana. Elizabeth maintained her commitment to the quality of Cynthiana hams through her tenure at Shakertown. In between adventures, Elizabeth continued to research, test, and develop recipes for the restaurant. One of the first immediate successes was the Shaker Lemon Pie, which Elizabeth adapted from *The Shaker Cook Book: Not by Bread Alone*, by Caroline B. Piercy. This dessert became highly successful and often requested. It became the first lettered calligraphy handout that would become available to customers over the years.

Shaker Lemon Pie

Have ready 2 uncooked piecrusts.

2 large lemons
2 cups sugar
4 eggs, well beaten

Slice lemons as thin as paper, rind and all, removing all seeds. Combine with sugar and mix well. Let stand for 5–7 hours, or preferably overnight, stirring occasionally.

Preheat the oven to 450°. Add beaten eggs to the lemon mixture and mix well. Turn into a 9-inch pie pan lined with pie pastry, and arrange the lemon slices evenly. Cover with top crust and crimp the edges. Cut several slits near the center. Bake for 15 minutes. Reduce heat to 375°, and bake for about 20 minutes or until a knife inserted near the edge of the pie comes out clean. Cool before serving.

Even as they were feeding the summer guests, Elizabeth was helping to design and equip the kitchen and dining rooms at the Trustees' Office, where the formal dining room would be. Early in the days between the closing of the summer kitchen and the opening of the main dining room area, Elizabeth began to plan her new, expanded menu. She wanted basic, simple cooking that was familiar in style to central Kentucky fare, but she also wanted to include some original Shaker recipes outside of the well-known Shaker lemon pie. She experimented with other recipes, like the Shaker chestnut omelet, but it was quickly abandoned. The original recipe called for two cups of flour, and the omelet came out of the oven dry with the consistency of corn bread! Elizabeth reflected that replicating and creating recipes for Shakertown was a major challenge. Since the Shakers didn't leave a cookbook, Elizabeth compiled recipes from a variety of sources. She used Pleasant Hill's old business records to look at Shaker sales of produce, canned goods, and seeds as well as their purchases of items like lemons and molasses. She also used journals, letters, and diaries to form a complete picture of what was served at Pleasant Hill, but she had to perfect how the food was actually prepared. Elizabeth used her own extensive collection of central Kentucky recipes, along with Caroline Piercy's *The Shaker Cookbook* and William L. Lassiter's *Shaker Recipes and Formulas for Cooks and Homemakers*.

The building that was to house the restaurant was the Trustees' Office. Built originally as a place where members of the Shaker community would interact with the public, it has a different look and feel than other Shaker buildings. After the Shaker era, the Trustees' Office was used as a guest house and then a privately owned restaurant. Constructed by Shaker brother Micajah Burnett, the building had twin spiral staircases opposite from one another in the main hall. The stairwells rose to a third floor, where there was a domed ceiling that captured the daylight and kept the area well illuminated. The restoration group was progressing with the project, and the Trustees' Office was the most qualified building to serve visitors with a dining area. It was decided that the restaurant would have five dining rooms, a kitchen to the rear, and a bakery and storage area in the basement. The dining rooms became known as the north, east, center, and south rooms. There was an additional spiral staircase to the basement as well as a spiral staircase at the rear of the side porch. The porch was counted as a dining room, as it had space to set eight tables of different sizes. This building was also to become home to Elizabeth for the next fifteen years.

Elizabeth had a room on the second floor of the Trustees' Office. It was one of the larger rooms midway to the back upstairs hall and had a bedroom and a bathroom. The bedroom was furnished with Shaker reproductions. She later moved across the hall to a suite of rooms, where she had a sitting room, a bathroom, and a bedroom, which meant she could move some of her furniture into the room.

James Cogar was the expert behind the dining room furnishings, table settings, handblown hurricane shades from Blenko in West Virginia, candles, and candlesticks. Jim also supervised the reproduction Shaker tables and chairs that were to be in the dining rooms as well as in every guest and living room.

When it came to uniforms for the servers and busboys at the Trustees' Office restaurant, Elizabeth and Jim decided the clothing should resemble traditional Shaker dress as much as possible. The busboys would wear a brown or dark blue smock made of hopsacking. This was an inexpensive but sturdy fabric that laundered easily. The servers would wear a simple, basic dress patterned after the Shaker fashion. They had three-quarter-length straight sleeves and hems to the base of the calf. A triangular white shawl and long white apron that was pinned at the waist would cover the dress and be stylish for any body type. Elizabeth chose a yellow gingham for herself and then later wore a brown and dark blue gingham. The Shakers wore gingham, and she also felt the pattern would show fewer food stains. The modern fabric was a permanent-press cotton that also laundered easily and required no ironing.

Much to everyone's delight, they found a small net Shaker cap in storage at the Center Family Dwelling. To Jim, this signified an authentic addition to the uniform, but to Elizabeth, it meant compliance with Kentucky health department laws that required hair to be covered in food service. Local seamstresses made all the uniforms.

Menus were to resemble journals handwritten by the Shakers, who kept daily journals in all their villages. It was decided that the menus would be in handwritten script resembling the simple form of the journal texts. The script minimized the swirly lines of both upper- and lowercase letters, and the font was large enough to be easily read. There were menus for daily midday fare and daily dinner fare, and they were printed on paper chosen by Jim that resembled an older type of bonded weight paper.

One of Jim's favorite recipes, which he served in his home to Elizabeth at dinner one evening, became part of the trustees' menu. It was an appetizer on the very first menu and was a long-lasting favorite.

Egg in Aspic on Anchovy Toast

1 teaspoon unflavored gelatin
½ cup cold water
1½ cups hot beef consommé (canned)
1½ teaspoons lemon juice
3 hard-boiled eggs, halved crosswise
Round toast
Anchovy paste

Soften gelatin by sprinkling it over ½ cup cold water. Pour hot consommé over this and mix. Add lemon juice and stir. Cool slightly and pour a small amount into individual molds, about ½ inch high. Small molds, about 1½ inches deep, are preferable. Place ½ hard-boiled egg, cut side up, into the liquid, and chill until consommé is firm. Then fill molds with cooled consommé mixture and chill. When firm, turn out on crisp round toast spread with anchovy paste. Garnish with a dressing made of mayonnaise thinned slightly with milk and seasoned with lemon juice and a scant drop of Tabasco sauce. The dish may also have a sprinkling of paprika.

Makes 6 servings. The toasts can be made ahead of serving by buttering slices of bread with a large biscuit cutter and toasting the slices on both sides. These may then be stored in tins. If the dish is on the soft side, it can be made more firm by adding a bit more gelatin.

Elizabeth wanted her restaurant customers to learn a bit about Shaker history while dining at the Trustees' Office, so she developed a table tent for customers to read and included a short newspaper article her father had written in "Cromwell's Comments," for the *Cynthiana Democrat* on May 29, 1930: "Here I recalled a most bountiful meal taken with the Shakers. In 1886, I happened to be one of a party of about a dozen wheelmen. After climbing the long hill, we were in a receptive mood for a square meal, and the hour being noon we decided to try our luck with the Shakers. Never shall I forget the meal we sat down to on that occasion. Like Oliver Twist, we asked for more, but unlike him, we were not denied."

By the beginning of April 1968, the staff, servers, and busboys were hired, and the housekeeping staff were ready to open. A small group of trustees were invited to participate in the launching of the village hospitality. They came to sleep in the beds and enjoy meals, and this allowed the new employees to have valuable training before they opened to the public.

The village restoration and the popular dining room were highly praised and as a result, visits by tourists and local residents began to increase. Magazines and newspaper articles helped spread the news, and by June, the Trustees' Office was full for most of its seatings.

Breakfast became the local residents' favorite meal, along with the overnight guests. The morning meal included scrambled eggs, bacon, sausage, country milk gravy, choice of in-season fruit, fruit juices, cereals, jellies, and marmalade. Hot biscuits and pumpkin or squash muffins were passed to the guests along with hot, freshly made coffee. Butter balls were abundantly placed on bread plates in front of the seated diners.

Squash Muffins

1 cup cooked mashed squash
½ cup brown sugar
½ cup molasses
½ cup soft butter
1 beaten egg
1¾ cups flour
1 teaspoon soda
¼ teaspoon salt
¼ cup pecans

Preheat the oven to 375°. Cook, drain, and mash squash to the consistency of mashed potatoes. Cream sugar, molasses, and butter. Blend in egg and squash and mix well. Combine flour, soda, and salt. Add flour mixture to the squash batter. Blend well and then fold in pecans. Fill well-greased muffin pans about half full with batter; bake for 20 minutes. Makes 1½ dozen.

This is an excellent recipe for people who don't like squash. The squash gives the batter the necessary consistency, but the flavor comes from the molasses.

Due to the crowds and popularity of breakfast, it could take some time for guests to receive their morning meals. Elizabeth, a constant perfectionist, was worried that this wait was unacceptably long. One evening before a busy weekend, she was sitting on the porch with her niece, Betty Morris, who was in charge of the business offices and inn, and some of her restaurant staff. In talking about how breakfast needed improvement, they decided that the Trustees' Office would host a country breakfast buffet. On the spot, they gathered a couple of busboys and servers and began to move the furniture around. They practiced "people movement" through the center dining room. They borrowed chafing dishes, Sterno heating cans, glass baking dishes, and various serving utensils from any employee who offered an ideal container.

The breakfast buffet was a huge success. One server and one busboy could handle the buffet line and keep it full of food while the other staff could take drink orders and keep the bread and coffee served to all the diners. By the following Monday morning, Betty and Elizabeth headed out to the restaurant supply store to purchase all the appropriate equipment.

Hot Curried Fruit

This recipe can be made with canned fruit halves.

>4 pear halves
>4 peach halves
>6 pineapple rings
>¼ cup brown sugar*
>½ teaspoon curry powder
>¼ stick butter

Preheat the oven to 400°. Drain juice from fruit. Place fruit, cut side up, in a shallow, buttered baking dish. Mix sugar and curry

---

* Good country sorghum molasses may be substituted for the brown sugar.

powder together, and sprinkle over fruit slices. Dot with butter. Bake until hot but not browned. Serve immediately.

If the seasonal fruit was not quite up to Elizabeth's standards, she would cut it up and add fresh lemon juice and a small amount of sugar to taste. This was tossed gently until the sugar was dissolved and gave a lift to otherwise dull fruit, saving money and eliminating waste.

Biscuits

1 cup flour
½ teaspoon salt
1½ teaspoons baking powder
3 tablespoons shortening
9 tablespoons milk

Preheat the oven to 425°. Sift dry ingredients in a large mixing bowl. Cut shortening into flour. Make a well in the center of the flour and put milk into the well. Stir until the dough cleans the bowl. Knead for ½ minute. Pat out the dough on a floured surface to about ½ inch or to desired thickness. Cut with a small biscuit cutter. Bake for 10 minutes or until golden brown. The cooked biscuits, once cooled, can be stored in a tin or frozen for later use.

Fried Apples

2 quarts small tart apples
½ cup brown sugar
½ cup white sugar

1 good pinch ground cinnamon
3 tablespoons butter

Leave skin on apples and cut each into 6 wedges. Remove cores and stems. Place apples in a heavy-bottomed skillet, sprinkle with sugars and cinnamon, and dot with butter. Cover with a lid and cook over low heat, turning apples if needed. Cook apples until they are tender but not mushy. Remove from heat when cooked and let stand for 3–5 minutes. Serve warm.

When tourism in Kentucky slowed down in the late fall and winter months, Sunday mornings were different at the Trustees' Office. Most of the staff were used to going to church on Sunday mornings, so they would alternate Sunday work shifts. The mornings that they were at work, they would hold a short worship service in the south room. Elizabeth loved this time, particularly the voices of the staff when they sang old hymns; she found it to be spiritually uplifting.

Baked Country Ham

Older hams—18 months or older—are the best for this recipe.

1 country ham
Water
¼ cup apple cider vinegar
½ cup brown sugar
1 teaspoon whole cloves

Scrub ham well to remove salt and any mold. Soak in water for 8 hours. Remove from the water and rinse off the ham. Preheat the oven to 350°. Place ham in the roaster and add enough water to slightly cover the ham. Add seasonings to the pan and place in the oven. Bake for 20 minutes per pound. An average-weight ham usually takes 4½ hours. Ham is done when bone is easily removed from the ham. Skin and bone ham; trim off excess fat. After this, the ham is ready for glazing.

Glaze for Ham

½ cup brown sugar
½ cup cornmeal
1 teaspoon ground cinnamon

Preheat oven to 350°. Mix ingredients together and smear over ham. Place in oven for 20 minutes. Wrap tightly in a gauze dish towel to pull ham back together. Cool in the refrigerator before slicing. When slicing, be sure portions are very thin.

Shakertown Fried Chicken

Iron skillets or very heavy-bottomed pans are best.

High-quality shortening
½ teaspoon salt
¼ teaspoon pepper
½ teaspoon paprika
2 cups flour
Whole chicken cut into quarters

Blend seasonings into flour in a paper bag. Then place chicken pieces, one at a time, in the bag and roll gently to fully coat the chicken. Place enough shortening in the skillet to be about ¼ inch deep. Chicken should be cooked over very low heat and turned only once to be sure not to lose crust. Cooking time is about 30 minutes, 15 minutes per side. Drain on a paper towel before serving.

Turkey Hash Griddle Cakes

1¾ cups turkey stock
1 teaspoon salt
Dash of pepper
Pinch red pepper
¼ cup flour blended with ½ cup cold water to make a paste
4 cups leftover turkey, cut into pieces
¼ cup onion, chopped
2 tablespoons butter

Heat butter in medium saucepan, add onion and cook until translucent. Add broth and seasonings and bring to boil. Gradually stir in flour paste. Stir constantly as mixture thickens, add turkey pieces and heat until turkey is hot. Set aside and keep warm until ready to serve on griddle cakes.

Griddle Cakes

1 egg
2 tablespoons oil
1 cup buttermilk
½ cup flour
1 cup plus 2 tablespoons cornmeal
½ teaspoon baking soda
½ teaspoon baking powder
3 teaspoons sugar
½ teaspoon salt
Milk to thin
1–2 tablespoons shortening or butter

Using a hand mixer, blend egg, oil, and buttermilk until smooth. On low speed, gradually blend dry ingredients. If the batter is too stiff, blend in enough milk to make the right consistency. Melt shortening on a griddle pan over low heat until it's hot. Pour out batter cakes to desired size (about ¼ cup). Fry slowly until the center shows bubbles and then flip. When browned on both sides, the cake should be done in the middle. Keep warm until ready to serve. Place on a platter, and serve hash in a small chafing dish placed on a plate beside the griddle cakes.

Pleasant Hill Salad Plate with Country Ham Biscuits and Chicken Salad

This entree was made up of a gelatin salad, chicken salad, country ham salad spread on warmed biscuits, and a few crisp chips.

Congealed Salad

1 cup boiling water
1 large package lemon gelatin dessert
2½ cups cold water
1 cup melon balls
1 can fruit cocktail, drained
1 cup white seedless grapes, sliced

Place boiling water in a bowl and add gelatin. Stir until dissolved; add cold water and stir until well blended. Put a small amount of mixed gelatin in a 9-by-13-inch glass dish, and place melon balls decoratively around the bottom of the dish. Place in the refrigerator and let set. Add the rest of the fruit gently; do not allow the dish to become warm; add the remaining gelatin dessert and return to the refrigerator. On a Tree of Life dinner plate[†] place the outer leaves of a head of lettuce on one side of the plate. Add about a cup of chicken salad to the lettuce, and garnish with a sprig of parsley. Place a side of fruit gelatin, topped with a daub of mayonnaise and a small sprig of parsley, beside the chicken salad. Place country ham biscuits on the plate across from the gelatin. Add a few fancy chips in the remaining space on the plate.

The salad plate gelatin varied seasonally and included an autumn salad, bing cherry salad, or Kentucky salad. This depended on what might be available from the garden or whether canned fruit was needed during the seasons where variety was limited.

Elizabeth asked for a small garden to be planted outside the Trustees' Office for "just a little parsley." This small garden turned into ten garden patches! The first crop of parsley was used up in two days, and much to Elizabeth's dismay, the garden could not raise enough parsley to keep up with the demand of her diners. But the gardens were a lovely feature for guests to look out on from the dining room windows. Staff and customers watched the first tomato grow and begin to turn red with much anticipation. One of the tourists brought it to the front desk so it would ripen.

Elizabeth would circulate through the dining rooms. One evening as a server was passing a glazed pineapple dish, the guest asked, "And do these grow in your garden?" The server replied, "Oh! Yes!" As Elizabeth overheard, she just cringed and ignored

---

[†] The Tree of Life plates were made exclusively for Pleasant Hill by Louisville Stoneware.

the exchange. Elizabeth was active in the restaurant, walking the floor, checking on the guests, or removing a salad dish or appetizer saucer from a table when she noticed they were empty.

Country Ham Biscuits

Preheat oven to 425°. Mix ground country ham with enough country dressing to produce a smooth consistency. Spread mixture on cooked biscuits. Heat for about 5 minutes or until very hot.

Chicken Salad

1 pound cooked chicken
¾ cup chopped celery
¼ teaspoon salt
¼ teaspoon black pepper
Dash of red pepper (optional)
1 part country dressing
2 parts mayonnaise
¼ cup chopped pecans (optional)
⅛ cup onion, diced (optional)

Cut chicken into cubes with scissors or a knife and mix with celery. Add seasonings and gently toss with a fork to coat the chicken mixture. Fold in country dressing. Add mayonnaise, pecans, and onions if using. Top with a bit more mayonnaise when serving.

Country Dressing

1 teaspoon dry mustard
2 tablespoons sugar
¼ teaspoon salt
2 tablespoons flour
½ cup cold water

2 egg yolks
¼ cup distilled white vinegar
2 tablespoons butter

Dissolve mustard, sugar, salt, and flour in ½ cup cold water. Beat egg yolks and vinegar in the top of a double boiler. Add dissolved ingredients and mix thoroughly. Cook and stir dressing over boiling water until thick and smooth. Add butter and stir.

Most restaurant managers are quick to align their practices with the requirements of the state health department to avoid any point deductions on their official monthly reports and evaluation. But Elizabeth was not the average restaurant manager.

Shakertown did receive demerits from the health department because she refused to comply as a matter of principle to some of their demands. The health department wanted all the silverware to be wrapped in napkins. Elizabeth refused, because proper table settings did not include wrapped silverware. Freshly pressed and folded linen napkins belonged flat on the table and not wrapped or rolled around the silverware. Elizabeth's staff, tables, and flatware were impeccable.

Another demerit came from Elizabeth's refusal to replace the sugar bowls with commercially packaged sugar packets that she knew would leave sugar trails and little piles of paper debris on the table. The staff would empty the sugar bowls and run them and their lids through the dishwasher every day. The bowls would be refilled the next morning and placed on the tables. Elizabeth believed that the bowls, kept covered on each table and emptied each evening for washing, presented a better table and met a higher public-health safety standard. Unfortunately, the health inspectors disagreed.

Elizabeth felt strongly about table presentation and took a firm stand in defense of her small, white cream pitchers. She willingly took the health department deductions to keep them in service. Elizabeth believed that the individually packaged cream containers that were recommended by the officials were nothing more than tabletop dairy advertisements, and she felt that advertising had no place on her customers' tables.

Elizabeth's standard of excellence extended to the financial aspects of her job, and she worked closely with the Shakertown financial department. She had them send her daily, weekly, and monthly reports so that she could adjust her food costs to the appropriate level. Her food costs were generally low, which consistently impressed Earl Wallace much as she had impressed R. M. Wheeler decades earlier.

Shakertown was in one of Kentucky's many dry counties, where the sale of alcohol was prohibited. However, some restaurants allowed customers to bring in alcoholic drinks from other counties. Elizabeth objected to this practice and argued to the trustees that most of her servers were under twenty-one and it was a poor example to have them witness their elders deliberately break the law.

By 1973, the dining rooms had served 850,000 guests; approximately 130,000 of those were overnight guests. Shakertown at Pleasant Hill was a huge success! Elizabeth believed that a good hostess should aim to please her guests, even when the Trustees' Office guest numbers reached the thousands. The local regulars who frequented the restaurant would often be pleasantly surprised to find that their favorite dishes were being served the day of their reservation. This surprise was no coincidence. Elizabeth would check the reservation list every day, and sometimes she would change a menu or add an entree on short notice to accommodate the Shakertown regulars.

Diners enjoying a meal in the Trustee's Office Dining Room. The servers, dressed in their period uniforms, are ready to make sure Elizabeth's standard of excellence is maintained, 1968. UKL, John C. Wyatt *Lexington Herald-Leader* Photographs, 2004av001.

The Shaker dining room attracted diverse palates and clientele, from government officials to local Little League coaches, film stars, senior citizens, busloads of tourists, food critics, and millionaires. No matter who the customers were, all were offered the same menus of standard daily fare, and it somehow managed to please all of them. Perhaps the Shakers themselves would have been pleased by the restaurant's success.

While Elizabeth demanded excellence from her employees, she did not encourage tipping at the restaurant. She felt that everyone worked as a team and equally as hard, whether the person was a server, a hostess, a cook, baker, busboy, dishwasher, or pot scrubber. Elizabeth knew that it took every one of the Trustees' Office's staff to get those meals on the tables every day. She treated all her employees as equals for whom she felt genuine concern. These people skills were not something that Elizabeth learned from a book but were reflected in her character, work ethic, and high standards.

Trustee's Office kitchen with a bountiful display of holiday dishes, including the Shaker Village corn sticks and locally grown vegetables, 1969. UKL, John C. Wyatt *Lexington Herald-Leader* Photographs, 2004av001.

Elizabeth would go over the recipes with her bakers, and she required that they get out their three-by-five recipe cards to follow along. She could tell by look and taste whether the recipe was being followed accordingly. It was not unusual to find Elizabeth in the basement bakery, reminding the baker to follow the measurements or instructions on the card. Elizabeth also knew that too much mixing and kneading of the biscuit or the pie dough would alter the lightness of the finished product, and with one bite, she would know what was done wrong. The bakery was where all those wonderful breads and desserts were created, and the marvelous smell from its ovens would fill the early morning air.

The Shakers were a self-sufficient community and had a storage area for their food. It was a very simple matter when the restoration was taking place to use all the areas of the Trustees' Office basement. Locker rooms, freezer and refrigeration room, deep sinks for pot scrubbing, an office for the food manager, and the bakery were all located in the basement.

Whole Wheat Rolls

2 tablespoons active dry yeast
2 cups lukewarm milk
1 egg, slightly beaten
½ cup granulated sugar
1 teaspoon salt
3½ cups wheat flour
1 cup plus 1 tablespoon shortening, melted
3½ cups all-purpose flour

Preheat oven to 400°. Dissolve yeast in lukewarm milk. Add egg, sugar, and salt. Stir in the whole wheat flour and then mix in shortening. Gradually add the white flour and work in a ball. Set aside and cover with a towel and let rise in a warm place until it doubles in size. Press down on the dough, cover, and let rise again until it doubles in size. Roll out on a floured board, cut with a biscuit cutter, and gently fold in a half circle, pinching edges lightly to seal. Place in a tubular pan or on a baking sheet and brush the top lightly with melted butter. Place in a warm spot, cover with a dampened towel, and let rise until it doubles in size. Bake for 12–15 minutes or until brown. These freeze well to serve later.

On April 3, 1974, central Kentucky and the surrounding states were hit by several tornadoes. This was before modern emergency warning signals. By word of mouth, the news was carried up from a radio located in the Trustees' Office basement. The dining room was crowded with guests and servers in various stages of meal service. Guests were being advised as to the weather conditions, and those who wished to seek shelter were helped down the narrow basement spiral staircases, while others continued to dine. One busboy came running up from the basement's pot-scrubbing sink in a panic. "Mrs. Kremer, Mrs. Kremer, the radio says I should take cover in the northwest corner of a basement," he shouted. Elizabeth calmly replied, "The pot room is in the northwest corner, go back to work." The sound of her voice along with her steadiness ended the panic.

Elizabeth was loyal to her employees, and most of them loved her dearly, but sometimes they still got furious with her, although never to her face. But they forgave her easily and generally listened to her suggestions. Elizabeth felt that all those who worked for her had potential, but she was stern with them over matters concerning their behavior. She wanted grace and dignity to serve as the public image. Joyce Murray, a longtime employee of Shakertown said, "I loved Mrs. Kremer dearly and we were friends, but I knew when it came to my hours on the clock, she expected certain ways for service to be conducted and that was the way I did my work." Elizabeth never raised her voice to shout, but she had a high-pitched, quick voice when she would make statements like "Oh! Don't do that" or "No! Not there" that made servers feel that they had committed an unpardonable sin. She definitely got one's attention even when she used her very low whisper voice close to the ear with statements like "Always remove the used dishes before bringing in a new serving!" Sometimes this statement was made as the server was delivering the new food, and Elizabeth would slip in beside the server and begin removing the dishes the server forgot. Elizabeth ran a tight ship!

First and foremost, Elizabeth wanted her customers to enjoy their dining experience, so she decided the meal should start with a relaxed mood. Medium and large wooden bowls were purchased for fresh vegetables. Small two-bowl pottery dishes with a loop handle were purchased from a Kentucky-owned potter called Bybee for the more liquid relishes. This way, guests could linger over the menu as long as they liked or needed and never feel rushed. All the while, they could snack on the vegetables or relishes set on each table.

Relish Bowl and Dish Contents

Green olives, both stuffed and with pits
Ripe olives, both pitted and with pits
Celery, both whole stalk and just center with leaves
Carrots, cleaned and cut into manageable strips
Pickled okra
Pickled corn, tiny shoots
Cherry tomatoes, in season
Onion, sliced rings, both fresh white and Spanish

Spring onion, in season
Sliced dill pickle
Bell pepper slices
Hot green peppers, small, about 4 to a bowl

Metal tongs were placed on top of the wooden bowls, and a small relish saucer was placed in front of each guest. The Bybee pottery bowls were also placed on the table and contained fresh corn relish, watermelon pickles, and sweet pickles. Relishes were passed continuously around the table. The point at which servers should ask guests if they were finished with the relishes before bringing in the other dishes for the main meal was a major decision.

Tomato celery soup was Elizabeth's creation, and with the capable skills of her cooks, Leona Bradshaw and Rose Yates, it became an all-time favorite. Elizabeth had the idea, and the three of them worked together to create a soup that was not only light enough to be served as an appetizer but also great to make ahead and be easily transported for special parties that were held in other locations at Pleasant Hill. Elizabeth recalled that the tomato soup gave her more trouble than any other recipe she developed for Shakertown. She knew from the Shaker records that they used tomatoes in a wide range of dishes, and she was determined to make a really good soup—and she did, "after endless pots of ordinary soup."

Tomato Celery Soup

2 tablespoons butter
1 small onion, chopped
½ cup celery, finely chopped
1 (10½ ounces) can tomato soup

1 soup can of water
1 tablespoon lemon juice
¼ teaspoon salt
1 teaspoon sugar
⅛ teaspoon pepper
Unsweetened whipped cream
1 teaspoon parsley, minced

Place butter in a medium saucepan and melt over low heat. Add onion and celery. Sauté lightly, the celery should remain crisp. Blend in tomato soup, water, and all other ingredients but the last two. Simmer for 5 minutes, stirring often. At the Trustees' Office, this was served topped with unsweetened whipped cream and a sprinkle of chopped parsley.

Vegetable Soup

4 quarts water
3½ cups fresh or canned tomatoes, chopped
3 carrots, sliced
2 stalks celery, thinly sliced
1 onion, chopped
2 cups green beans
2 medium boiling potatoes, cut into chunks
1 tablespoon salt
1 teaspoon sugar
¼ teaspoon ground cloves
1 teaspoon pepper
1 cup barley

Place water and tomatoes in a large soup pot; add carrots, celery, and onion. Cook for 40 minutes until carrots are tender. Stir in remaining ingredients and seasoning. Continue to cook for 1 hour.

Add in barley, stirring well and cooking until barley is done. Soup meat may be added to this recipe. Cook the meat for about 3 hours in the water. Add vegetables and seasoning when meat is tender. Add barley at the end of the cooking time.

Iced Potato Soup

6 medium russet potatoes, peeled and chopped
4 cups chicken broth
1 medium onion, chopped
2 tablespoons butter
1 teaspoon salt
1½ to 2 cups cream
Red pepper or Tabasco

Cook potatoes in chicken broth until tender. Sauté onion in butter until tender and set aside. Add onion and butter to potatoes. Season with salt. Cool slightly before placing in a blender—or use a sieve if a blender is not available. Blend soup in small amounts to prevent overflow. Chill. When ready to serve, add cream. Season with red pepper or Tabasco and taste for more salt. If served hot, heat soup and add warm cream.

Keep in mind, the next time you buy whole chickens, to freeze the uncooked necks, wings, and backs. When you have time, make your own stock from the scrap chicken. Place the scraps in a pot and add enough water to cover. Add celery leaves, parsley, salt, and pepper. Cook until meat falls from the bone. Strain and store in the freezer or refrigerator for just such recipes.

For Elizabeth, the Trustees' Office was her restaurant and home, but it became grandmother's house to John and Evalina (Kremer)

Settle's daughter, Anna. Elizabeth was an official resident of Pleasant Hill and, in 1969, its only registered voter. Much like Elizabeth's experience working at Jewell's Tea Room, Anna spent her high school and college summers working as a waitress and hostess at Shakertown. She tried to refer to Elizabeth as Mrs. Kremer, but she didn't always succeed. By the end of the summer, many of the servers and busboys would refer to their boss, only out of earshot, as "Grandmother."

But Elizabeth did feel that her employees were family. If she knew that they were having problems with car repairs, sick children, or even abuse, she would advise them and find them help. Elizabeth would advance pay for car repairs and make sure that no one would miss their high school prom!

Shakertown hosted the Kentucky Republican Governors' wives during Governor Nunn's administration. Anna was a hostess during that time. Elizabeth had formally been introduced to all the wives and was determined that her granddaughter meet Nancy Reagan. As she toured the dining room with Anna at her side, she stopped at a table and said, "Mrs. Reagan, I would like you to meet my granddaughter, Anna." Instantly worrying that she would slight the other women seated at the table, she said, "Anna, this is Nancy Reagan," and turning to the other woman nearby, she asked, "And what was your name?" The woman smiled and said, "Mrs. Rockefeller." The family never let Elizabeth forget that one!

Elizabeth knew that the surest way to command the respect of her employees was to deserve it. She encouraged each member of her team, whether a dishwasher or a server, to be an equally important part of the group and to be respected as an individual. Mutual respect produced the framework that supported the restaurant at Pleasant Hill and allowed it to emerge as a landmark in food service quality. Elizabeth created an environment where the employees took as much pride in the Trustees' Office as she did.

Elizabeth really did become like a grandmother to some of her staff. Many of them were young, and it was easy to see her that way, especially since her grandchildren were ever present in the restaurant—although the family (and likely many of the employees) felt that Elizabeth's true power and authority in management came from her shoes! Many a time, an entire roomful of restaurant employees would literally jump to attention and spring into action at the sound of her heels clicking on the hardwood floor. Elizabeth had a distinctive walk, so recognizable that her employees learned the sound of her step long before they learned to work the ancient punch-type time clock in the basement.

The south room, used often as a break room, was two large dining rooms away from Elizabeth's office. This location was a safe distance from the main dining room to allow socializing without being seen or heard by the boss. It was a favorite place for kitchen workers, servers, busboys, stock workers, hostesses, and bakers to chat, as all its entrances and stairways opened into that one room. It was a favorite place of Elizabeth's family as well. Anna recalled that it was the room where she learned how to fold napkins properly, roll butter balls on wooden paddles, make melon balls without wasting any of the melon, the trick to pinning a shawl and apron, and the power of the sound of Elizabeth's shoes. The crowd would gather in the south room, where they couldn't see Elizabeth or hear her voice. But even above the din of their carefree conversation, they knew in two clicks if the sound of footsteps belonged to Elizabeth, and they would all scatter like mice. Anna remembered that she would even scatter with them! She wondered if maybe Elizabeth would simply open her office door and take a couple of steps and return to her desk, knowing exactly what effect the noise would have on the south room. Anna certainly suspected that she did! The authority found in those shoes and her walk eliminated the need for a commanding voice, a stern face, or intimidating eyes. In fact, those shoes were Elizabeth's most valuable tool.

A special challenge to the restaurant manager lies in creating those extra touches that offer guests a memorable and unique dining experience. During Elizabeth's time at Shakertown, her willingness to meet those challenges and ensure she was providing her diners with signature touches are what brought them all back again and again.

Serving butter balls was a marvelous excuse to indulge oneself with a bit of butter on a "melt in your mouth" roll. The butter balls were fascinating for the younger guests, an attractive addition to the table, and a way to keep the servers close to their guests. It would give them an opportunity to check on their guests and be attentive without being too pushy.

Taking a pat of butter and rolling it in the palm of one's hand, chilling it in ice water and then rolling it quickly between two grooved paddles became a tool. Rolling butter allowed breakfast staff time to catch up, relax, and gossip with one another. But it also avoided labor gaps before lunch service began. Young Anna loved this job. As a girl, she most enjoyed the stray butter ball occasionally launched by workers having a bit of fun and the accompanying return fire. The butter rollers did limit their ball tossing to the ones that had unintentionally dropped prior to the launch, taking advantage of an accident and turning it into a game. In this way, making butter balls became an event instead of a task that left everyone feeling a bit more like true Shakers with a little more pride when guests would gush over the unctuous creations.

The small touches made a difference. The little details like serving small, ridged balls of butter served individually with a spoon, folded cloth napkins, parsley, mint, Bibb lettuce, lemon, or red pepper garnishes arranged on or in nearly everything, lighted candles in the evenings, servers in their dining costumes reflecting back a mood, and all the well-trained serving staff created a lasting experience for the guests. All these touches became synonymous with the restaurant and left critics and fans alike with hopeful expectations of great things to come.

Speaking of garnishes, they were important to Elizabeth, but she never wanted them to dominate the food. The reason she chose the Tree of Life plate was that it had the tree in the center, which gave the appearance of a hub where the foods made up the spokes of the wheel. Parsley and mint were her favorite garnishes for eye appeal. She thought they added a dash of color and design to the presented food. Leaf lettuce was her choice for the base of a food. She also believed that garnishes added a touch of class and gave the impression of a better value for your money. She had the food at the Trustees' Office dressed with her favorites, but she also directed her cooks to use a pat of butter sprinkled with salt and pepper placed under any grilled steak that was served. One favorite recipe remembered by many from both the early days and more recently was the Scalloped Oyster Plant.

Scalloped Oyster Plant (Salsify)

Canned salsify may be purchased.

> 3 cups oyster plant, sliced
> 2 cups saltine cracker crumbs
> 1½ teaspoons salt
> ½ teaspoon paprika
> 4 tablespoons butter
> 3 cups cream
> Buttered bread crumbs

Preheat oven to 400°. In a saucepan, heat the salsify and cook until tender. If using canned, skip this step. Slice the salsify into bite-size pieces. In a greased baking dish, layer cracker crumbs and then oyster plant. Add seasoning and dots of butter to each layer. Pour cream about 1 inch deep into the casserole. Top with buttered bread crumbs. Bake for about 30 minutes.

Buttered Bread Crumbs

3 slices stale bread, crust removed, diced
2 tablespoons butter

Melt the butter in a saucepan. Add diced bread pieces and stir over medium-high heat until the bread absorbs the butter and begins to toast. When golden brown, remove from the heat and set aside until ready to use.

Many people who lived close to the village made the Trustees' Office a weekly visit, especially in the winter. If the weather would turn nasty, locals would head there because it felt like going to "Mom's house." One customer remembered that they would cater to his requests even on holidays. Elizabeth would see his name in the reservation book and let the kitchen know he was coming. Each time, he ordered tomato celery soup with no whipped cream or garnish and a plain, county ham sandwich—nothing spread on the bread slices.

When Elizabeth was in her seventies, she fell and broke her arm but was back to work as soon as she got bored with sitting around, which did not take long. She did need to have some help going down the staircases, but as soon as her shoe hit the floor after the bottom step, you could hear a pin drop. All the staff knew she was on the floor and ready to work. It made a difference in their job knowing she was only an upstairs ring away.

Myrl and Mary Schnake would come down annually from Illinois and spend several days in the village. Elizabeth would often visit with them in the evening. A letter from the Schnake family expressed their feelings about Elizabeth and Shakertown: "She [Elizabeth] was always concerned about pleasing the people who ate in the dining room, her standards were high, and she let her staff know they were high. I once heard one of the servers in the back room telling a second server, 'Don't let Mrs. Kremer catch you doing that. This is supposed to be a high-class place.' Your mother had at least one believer."

Myrl recalled that Elizabeth wanted a gardener who could grow small potatoes. After the tenure of the former gardener, Mr. King, the other gardeners let the potatoes get too large for her to use, and Elizabeth was *not* happy about it. The small potatoes were boiled and served with a dollop of butter, and she felt rather strongly that the large potatoes were too common and bland. Elizabeth had high standards and was known to run the kitchen "without wasting a bean." Another product that disappointed Elizabeth was the whipping cream; it did not meet her standards and she consistently bemoaned its poor quality. "Stuff now is so processed you often wonder if it has ever been inside a cow," Elizabeth said. Even the milkman knew of her dissatisfaction and would let her know at the holiday season when he had cream "that wasn't doctored up."

She hated serving milk in small, packaged cartons rather than bringing a full glass to the dining guests. But the health department required the use of milk cartons, and Elizabeth compensated by scouring the dining rooms for empties as soon as they were finished. She couldn't stand for people to eat with trash on their tables. While there may have been nothing she could do about the health regulations, she could at least make sure the guests didn't have to sit with trash for too long.

Myrl and Mary remembered clearly how Elizabeth was always present in the dining room, checking, looking around, and generally just being in charge. Elizabeth was the manager, and she wanted the dining room to be the best it could be. Putting in long, tedious hours, her dedication was admirable, and the food service and the dining room reflected her time and effort and her desire to do the best that she could.

The Schnakes used the standard of excellence they experienced at Shaker Village as their baseline for any other restaurant experience. Any praise or even complaint was based on whether Elizabeth would have approved or disapproved of the service or food that they had just had. Her standard in the dining room was the rule they used to judge quality.

After they had been going to Shakertown for a couple of years, they made a reservation and then got a return phone call about a half hour after making the reservation. It was Elizabeth on the phone asking if there was anything Myrl would particularly enjoy having while they were there. This personal touch was why they liked visiting so much. Elizabeth's staff were friendly and made the Schnakes feel like they were visiting their own family and not just vacationing.

Tomato Okra Casserole

6 tablespoons onions, chopped
2 tablespoons bacon grease
1 pound okra, sliced
1 quart tomatoes, peeled and cooked, or canned
¼ teaspoon curry powder
½ teaspoon paprika
1 tablespoon sugar
1½ teaspoons salt

¼ teaspoon red pepper
2½ tablespoons Parmesan cheese
8 butter crackers, crumbled

Preheat oven to 350°. Sauté onions in bacon grease. Add okra and cook until tender. Add tomatoes and seasoning. Pour into a greased casserole dish. Top with cheese and then cracker crumbs. Bake for 35 minutes. Serves about 12.

Broccoli Casserole

2 cups cut broccoli or a 10-ounce package, frozen
¼ pound Velveeta cheese
4 tablespoons butter, divided
12 butter crackers, crumbled

Preheat oven to 350°. Cook and drain broccoli (if using frozen, let thaw). Melt cheese with half of butter. Mix with broccoli and place in a greased baking dish. Melt remaining butter and mix with crumbled crackers. Sprinkle additional crumbs on top of the casserole dish. Bake for about 20 minutes. This casserole can be made the day before serving and refrigerated. Add cracker crumbs on top just before baking.

Lemon-Glazed Carrots

1 quart fresh small carrots[‡]
2 tablespoons light brown sugar
⅓ cup granulated sugar
2 teaspoons lemon juice
2 tablespoons butter

[‡] At Shakertown, they purchased tiny canned Belgian carrots when fresh vegetables were unavailable.

Preheat oven to 450°. Wash and clean carrots and cook until tender; do not overcook. Drain carrots and place in a baking dish. Keep warm and set aside until ready to bake. Just before serving, combine the sugars and sprinkle over the carrots. Add lemon juice and dot with butter. Bake for about 20 minutes and serve immediately.

Coconut Cream Tarts

¼ cup granulated sugar
¼ cup plus 1 tablespoon flour
¼ teaspoon salt
2 cups milk
2 egg yolks beaten with ¼ cup sugar
1 tablespoon butter
1 teaspoon vanilla
Baked tart shell
Unsweetened whipped cream
Shredded coconut

Combine sugar, flour, and salt in a double boiler. Slowly stir in milk. Cook over boiling water until the mixture is thick like a custard. Cover and cook 12 minutes longer, stirring occasionally. Beat egg yolks into the ¼ cup sugar. Stir a little of the hot custard into the mixture to temper the eggs, and then pour the egg mixture into the custard. Cook for about 2 minutes or until thick. Remove from heat and add butter and vanilla. Blend well and then cool. Pour into a baked tart shell and top with unsweetened whipped cream. Sprinkle generously with coconut when ready to serve.

Oatmeal Pie

¾ cup granulated sugar
¾ cup corn syrup
6 tablespoons butter
2 eggs, beaten slightly
1 teaspoon vanilla
¾ cup quick rolled oats, uncooked
Unbaked pie shell

Preheat oven to 350°. Mix together the granulated sugar, corn syrup, and butter. Fold in slightly beaten eggs. Add the vanilla and mix well. Stir in the oats and pour in an unbaked pie shell. Bake for 30–35 minutes.

Kremer friends and family became frequent visitors to Shakertown. One of Elizabeth's friends laughingly stated, "My daughter owes all her cooking abilities to 'my mama's mama, my dad's mama, and Elizabeth Kremer.'" As Elizabeth established herself at the Trustees' Office and the dining room became popular, Evalina and Pem's childhood friends discovered the peaceful joys of Shakertown.

The overnight accommodations were reasonable for families, and the luxuries of the village after the exhibits closed were unbelievable. Children could walk and run around the village until they were exhausted for bedtime. The adults could sit and rock in the sitting rooms outside the bedrooms, knowing their children were close by. For many years, those old friends came to gather and spend New Year's Eve and Day at Shakertown.

The friends all stayed in the same building and had the last dinner of the year together. Some years, up to eight families would come from West Virginia, Louisville, South Carolina, and

Indiana. It was great fun for everyone, and Elizabeth particularly loved it. She loved to have all the grown-up girls from past slumber parties and weekend sleepovers in her life again. Elizabeth would try to have the Shaker dish of the day be a girls' request. One of the childhood visitors, Pat, asked Elizabeth why she didn't offer fried gizzards as the Shaker dish of the day, because her family loved gizzards. Elizabeth asked Pat to stop by her office before the family headed back home, where she gave Pat a package wrapped in numerous layers of newspaper to keep everything frozen until the visitor reached Louisville. When Pat got home, she had five hundred gizzards for her freezer!

Another childhood friend, Betsy from South Carolina, would come to the village every year for New Year's Eve. After one overnight stay at Shakertown, she went to Elizabeth's office to say goodbye. She was carrying an empty pie pan from the year before. Elizabeth promptly replaced it with a new pie pan filled with a fresh Shaker lemon pie. If Betsy didn't bring the empty one back, Elizabeth wouldn't give her a new pie to take home!

Every year, one of the girls made the bourbon ball recipe from the *Welcome Back to Pleasant Hill* cookbook. This was a staple of the New Year's celebration, and other friends made their own recipes.

Kentucky Bourbon Balls

½ cup butter
3½–4 cups powdered sugar
4 tablespoons or less bourbon
Pecans for topping the balls
4 squares semisweet chocolate
¼ bar paraffin

Cream the butter and add the sugar gradually, blending well. Slowly add the bourbon and blend thoroughly. Chill for about

1 hour or more. Roll in 1-inch balls and place on waxed paper. Lightly press a pecan on top. Chill for 1 hour or more. On top of a double boiler, melt chocolate and paraffin and stir to blend. Dip in balls with a three-pronged fork and return to waxed paper. Chill. Store in tins in the refrigerator until serving.

With all her success both personally and professionally, not a day went by that Elizabeth didn't mention how much Doc would have loved seeing Shakertown restored. He would have loved getting into the buildings and checking out the construction. She missed him, but his spirit was with her. Evalina and Pem knew that he would have most loved to know that Elizabeth had succeeded in creating another popular restaurant. He would have been so proud.

The Trustees' Office was lovely in the evenings. The walls held round Shaker candle sconces with simple black candlesticks that were wired with small electric bulbs, resembling the candles on the tables. One of the many gifts that Shakertown gave to Elizabeth was the peace and serenity of its evenings. Unlike in other jobs, where you would leave at the end of your shift and fight your way home in traffic, Elizabeth could simply move to the porch, have a light supper, and enjoy her evening. Her staff knew that at the end of a hectic day, Elizabeth loved to have a bowl of dry cereal with a pitcher of cold cream, a piece of homemade loaf bread lightly toasted and buttered and wrapped in a cloth napkin to keep it warm, and a piece of in-season fresh fruit. She would have her evening meal with the few employees left on duty, and as she finished her dinner, they would check in with her on some of the next day's needs. Giving the dining room an approving glance and checking at the front desk for the time of her wake-up call, she would start her ascent up the spiral staircase. Always taking the time to say goodnight to any overnight guests as they were

Elizabeth walking through the Shaker Village of Pleasant Hill. UKL, Elizabeth Kremer Cromwell Papers, 2016ms043.

heading up to their rooms, Elizabeth Cromwell Kremer was one of the last to experience the full extent of the Shaker spirit of simplicity and excellence at Pleasant Hill.

Elizabeth Cromwell Kremer is part of the Shakertown story, blending perfectly with its beauty, its charm, its heart of elegant simplicity, and its spirit of hospitality. A small-town Kentucky girl whose fierce determination led to her success in the restaurant industry, Elizabeth lived as she worked—with excellence. In November 1970, Elizabeth put together a small recipe book, *We Make You Kindly Welcome*, with the editorial assistance of her daughters Pem and Evalina. The phrase "we make you kindly welcome" was the greeting offered by the Shaker sisters to their dinner guests. Published by Pleasant Hill Press, a small book of recipes that were widely enjoyed by Shaker guests is still sold in the gift shop today. The menu book was organized to follow the menu of the Trustees' Office dining room, with specials from morning through evening. The book contains 290 recipes, including hominy grits casserole, chicken croquettes, Shaker lemon pie, and pumpkin muffins. Along with the recipes is a brief history of Shaker Village and an explanation of their tradition of excellence. Elizabeth's daughter Evalina sketched drawings of Shaker dishes and kitchen utensils to illustrate the cookbook.

In the March 1976 issue of *Bon Appetit* magazine, in a continuing series on regional American food specialties, Jane P. Fowler highlighted American cooking from Kentucky's Bluegrass country. In a beautiful, full-color spread, the article highlights Harrodsburg's Beaumont Inn and the restaurant at Shakertown. In describing the restaurant and dining experience, Fowler calls out Elizabeth Kremer as "the essence of the well-bred Southern hostess." She noted how attentive and courteous the servers were, behavior that Elizabeth expected from her staff. Among the multitude of dishes that Fowler recommended were the squash muffins, tomato and celery soup, the relish bowl, the incredible breakfast dishes, and certainly the Shaker lemon pie. Another recurring theme was carrying on the Shaker tradition of using fresh herbs, fruits, and vegetables.

In 1977, Elizabeth published her second cookbook, *Welcome Back to Pleasant Hill: More Recipes from the Trustees' House*. For this volume, Elizabeth compiled additional recipes that she used in the Shakertown daily menus as well as her favorite dishes from family and friends.

In 1981, Shaker Village caught the attention of *New York Times* food editor, Craig Claiborne, who was in Kentucky to serve as judge for the March of Dimes Gourmet Gala at the Hyatt-Regency. Craig and other guests were treated to lunch at Shakertown. Claiborne requested a taste of Kentucky foods during his visit to Lexington, so he was treated to chilled pea soup, corn sticks, coleslaw, Pleasant Hill chicken, corn pudding, baked tomatoes, and old ham (from Cynthiana), along with chess pie, Shaker lemon pie, and rhubarb pudding. Claiborne asked Elizabeth where chess pie got his name. While she admitted that she couldn't figure it out either, she relayed this story to the New York food editor. She told him that one day, she and her husband had stopped at a small country restaurant in Tennessee whose owner explained that "when there's no apples and no cherries, they have chess pie." One popular origin story of chess pie attributes the name to a variation of "it's just pie" that combined with a classic Southern drawl became "it's jes pie" which later became "it's chess pie."

Chess Pie

½ cup butter, melted
1½ cups sugar
3 eggs

1½ teaspoons cornmeal
1½ teaspoons vinegar
1 unbaked piecrust

Preheat the oven to 450°. Over low speed, mix butter and sugar until just combined. Add eggs, one at a time, mixing between additions. Add cornmeal and vinegar and mix until just blended. Place piecrust in a 9-inch pan and crimp edges. Pour in filling and place in the oven. Immediately turn the oven down to 400° and cook for 15 minutes. Then turn oven down to 300° and bake for 20 minutes more. The filling should puff up. Jiggle the pie to make sure the filling is set before removing it from the oven. Place on a rack to cool.

Corn Sticks

½ teaspoon salt
½ teaspoon baking soda
3 teaspoons sugar
½ teaspoon baking powder
2 tablespoons oil
1 egg
½ cup flour
1 cup buttermilk
1 cup plus 2 tablespoons cornmeal

Preheat oven to 450°. Beat all ingredients together until well mixed. Heat greased cast-iron corn pans until hot enough to sizzle in contact with water. Fill irons halfway. Bake for 10 minutes or until brown.

Corn sticks, prepared in their specialized cast-iron dish, 1969. UKL, John C. Wyatt *Lexington Herald-Leader* Photographs, 2004av001.

In the January/February 1981 issue of *Americana* magazine, Gail King published "Cooking the Shaker Way," and highlighted the history of Shakertown, the food, and, of course, Elizabeth Kremer. The article conveys Elizabeth's commitment to fresh, nutritious food in a hospitable setting. In discussing the way food was served, Elizabeth said, "Food is best when it pleases the eye as well as the appetite." The article also manages to demonstrate Elizabeth's expectations for excellence: "Elizabeth can tell at a glance if a fork is out of place. . . . Mrs. Kremer's cooks declare that she can detect an extra speck of salt in a pot of beans."

When John Egerton published *Southern Food: At Home, on the Road, in History*, he found key information in Kentucky cookbooks, among them, *We Make You Kindly Welcome*, by Elizabeth Kremer. In an interview for the *Lexington Herald-Leader*, he said, "Kentucky has a richer food history than any other state in the South except Louisiana. Kentucky's is longer and more continuous." Regarding southern food history, he said, "Food really is a part of us. There's nothing else in our culture as strong and enduring in our memories as food. We appreciate it through all five of our senses."

In 1983, Earl Wallace proclaimed that Elizabeth had served her 2 millionth meal—a truly impressive number for a woman who came out of retirement to work at Shakertown. With a long career behind her, Elizabeth semiretired in 1986, turning over most of the director's duties to Jack Leonard, assistant vice president of food services. Elizabeth belonged to a group of women who fit somewhere between the domestic housewife and the feminist generation. They were often pioneers in their fields: southern women with a sense of family and place, with definite ideals concerning behavior and family. They often had a flair for exploration and adventure, yet also a sense of heritage and history. They came of age into their careers in the 1920s, and many opted both for a career and family. They demonstrated that it was possible to do both. These brilliant and ambitious women paved the way for generations to follow.

After a brief illness, Elizabeth passed away on September 26, 1988. Elizabeth Cromwell Kremer was a daughter, wife, mother, and restaurant manager. She broke norms, learned from her mistakes, and lived and worked hard. Among Elizabeth's numerous achievements, she played a key role in revitalizing Shakertown as a tourist destination, in establishing its culinary history, and in allowing her spirit of excellence and simplicity to endure beyond her life.

Epilogue

Around 1935, Elizabeth gave the following speech to the Ohio
Restaurant Association in Cincinnati, Ohio.

Restaurant work is essentially a woman's field.

Long before women became associated with the
business world, it was her job to prepare or supervise
the preparation of food and to create that attractive
and restful atmosphere which is the true meaning of
hospitality.

We might say, in the terms of this radio age, a
restaurant is an amplified home. This, in part, has en-
abled women to bring into the restaurant business a
certain attention to detail and to those niceties of service which have gained for them a recognition in this
industry.

I believe that women have encountered less op-
position in the restaurant business than in any other
field into which they have ventured. That this is true
is evidenced by the fact that the advertising policies of
some of the larger restaurants feature the slogan "We
have only women supervisors and women cooks."

It is also of interest to note how many positions in
restaurants, cafeterias, and hotels are held by women.
Sometimes, I think that the encroachment of women

in the restaurant is similar to the fable of the Arab and the camel. The camel first stuck his nose into the tent begging for just a little shelter and, bit by bit, gradually edged in until he had occupied the entire tent. Woman's first entrance into "the restaurant" was as a waitress. She gradually assumed the responsibility for the supervision of food, and she soon demonstrated her ability to manage and own the restaurant successfully. . . .

Restaurant work differs from most other businesses in that your schedule is counterclockwise to the average person's schedule. Your hours are topsy-turvy. You are serving dinner when everyone else is going home from their day's work. You are busiest when others relax from the tension of the day. In fact, other people's holidays are your headaches.

In connection with these headaches, I have learned from experience that I should have supplemented my course in institutional management with practical training in plumbing and electrical installations and elementary knowledge of law, particularly garnishee laws and court procedure, the fundamentals of fire prevention and first aid, and by all means, learned how to maintain cordial relations with the police department so that I could get my cooks out of jail in time for Sunday dinner.

I hope that you who are planning to enter the restaurant field are not being disillusioned, for truly it is a most interesting and fascinating work, which offers a wide scope of opportunity.

I can assure you, at least, that even if sometimes it is a headache, it is never a bore.

Afterword

Every time I took a break from the pages of this book, my mind would wander to an old saying—"A woman's place is in the kitchen"—once meant to demean and relegate women to domestic duties and exclude them from executive ones. It referred to the home kitchen, of course. The work of a restaurant kitchen was too intellectual, too emotionally taxing, too physically demanding for the "weaker sex."

Elizabeth Kremer would have none of that attitude. The vivid stories and delicious narratives Deirdre has shared in these pages started to bring an entirely new meaning to the expression as I began to feel a profound connection to Elizabeth.

Pioneering and headstrong, this unflappable Kentucky woman likely never knew the impact she would have on the lives of female chefs generations later. As I grew to know more of her life, "a woman's place is in the kitchen" began to ring true, its negative connotations fading away. My kitchen is my studio, my pots and pans my canvas, my dishes my masterpieces. I am strong enough for its demands both mental and physical. As I follow Elizabeth's lead in dismantling the preconceived notions about restaurant work being man's work, I, too, set an example for my own daughters and for all women who work to tear down sex-based barriers in any workplace.

In these pages, I started to see Elizabeth as a spiritual forebear. I felt proud at her accomplishments, achieved during a time where so few pathways for women had been paved. I rejoiced at her stubborn insistence on bucking tradition in both how she lived and how she cooked. I salivated at her recipes. My restaurant, freight house, sits on the same river where she met her husband; my town, Paducah, still bears scars from the 1937 Ohio River flood that badly damaged her Louisville restaurant, French Village.

Not only did Elizabeth ignore the limitations society attempted to place on women, but she also ignored conventions about age, opening a new restaurant at sixty-five and publishing two cookbooks into her seventies. This "well-bred Southern hostess" never stopped creating, never stopped learning, and in this, she set an example we all should strive to emulate. Elizabeth Cromwell Kremer is essential to the history of Shaker Village and Kentucky, and I'm grateful for Deirdre's work in compiling these details about her rich life.

sara bradley
the freight house
chef/proprietor

Acknowledgments

I would like to thank Evalina Settle for entrusting me with the initial manuscript, *Her Story*, and her husband, John, for answering all my questions along the way. I'm grateful to the University of Kentucky Libraries Special Collections Research Center staff, especially Sarah Coblentz, and the student assistants who regularly retrieved my research materials. I want to thank Reinette Jones for trying her best to help me unravel the history of Cuz, even though it remains incomplete. I am fortunate to work with wonderful individuals who inspire and support me. My coworker and friend, Shawn Livingston, is a fountain of excellent ideas and gave me the best ones throughout this project! I am so honored and humbled that Ouita Michel and sara bradley, two incredible women and chefs, contributed to this book. As always, I am so thankful to my family and friends, who continue to put up with me, especially Ryan Smith, Dean McMahan, Rebekah Reeves, and Shanna Wilbur. Speaking of family, my grandmother, Dorothy Wilson, has long been my inspiration to live as a strong, independent woman. She was the center of our family gatherings and meals, an amazing cook, gardener, and the woman who taught me that there wasn't a limit on what I could achieve.

Selected Resources

Cooper, Dorothea C. *Kentucky Hospitality: A 200-Year Tradition*. Louisville: Kentucky Federation of Women's Clubs, 1976.

Fowler, Jane P. "American Cooking from Kentucky's Bluegrass Country." *Bon Appetit*, March 1976, 24–29.

King, Gail. "Cooking at Shakertown: Taste and Nutrition." *Americana*, January/February 1981, 32–37.

Kremer, Elizabeth C. *Welcome Back to Pleasant Hill*. Harrodsburg, KY: Pleasant Hill Press, 1977.

Kremer, Elizabeth C., and Evalina K. Settle. *We Make You Kindly Welcome*. Harrodsburg, KY: Pleasant Hill Press, 1970.

Parrish, Thomas. "A Fantastic Accomplishment." In *Restoring Shakertown: The Struggle to Save the Historic Shaker Village of Pleasant Hill*, 94–111. Lexington: University Press of Kentucky, 2005. http://www.jstor.org/stable/j.ctt2jcq8h.14.

Primary Sources from the University of Kentucky Libraries Special Collections Research Center

Clay Lancaster Kentucky Architectural Photographs, 2014av001

Elizabeth Cromwell Kremer Papers, 2016ms043

Frances Jewell McVey Papers, 0000ua003

Glass Plate Negative Collection, 2007ua014

Jewell Family Papers, 2011ms063

John C. Wyatt *Lexington Herald-Leader* Photographs, 2004av001
John M. Cromwell Scrapbooks, 2014ms095
Kentuckian Yearbooks
Lafayette Studios Photographs, 96pa101
Louis Edward Nollau F Series Photographic Print Collection, 1998ua001

Index of Recipes

ambrosia, 24
angel food cake, 52–53; Elizabeth's instant, 157–58
Anna's French dressing, 140
apple(s): dumpling, 91; fried, 174–75
apricot cream cheese spread, 65
arroz con pollo, 27–28
artichokes, 128
asparagus: arroz con pollo, 27–28; marinated, 154
avocado: fruit salad, 28–29; gazpacho, 26–27; grapefruit and avocado salad, 140

bacon buns, 135
baked: bean soup, 83–84; country ham, 175–76; fish, 27; ham with mustard sauce, 60–61; spam with pineapple, 108
baking powder biscuits, 8
banana peanut butter salad, 87
basic: cream sauce, 93–94; white sauce, 96–97, 155–56
beaten biscuits, 21

beef: creamed chipped beef, 54; meat loaf, 84; pot roast, 75; spaghetti Italian, 141; Swiss steak, 85
Benedictine spread, 65
beverages: daiquiri, 77–78; hot cocoa with marshmallows, 133–34; lime drink, 29; mint julep, 78; spiced tea, 42; we three ice, 43
biscuits: 174; baking powder, 8; beaten, 21; old recipe beaten, 21
bittersweet chocolate-peppermint wafers, 61
boiled dressing, 56
bread(s): corn sticks, 206; French Village rolls, 71; ginger bread, 46–47; icebox rolls, 17–18; Parker House rolls, 130–31; squash muffins, 172; whole wheat rolls, 185–86
breaded pork chops, 140–41
broccoli casserole, 198
broiled quail, 18
brown sugar sauce, 46–47
buttered bread crumbs, 195

217

cabbage: coleslaw, 55–56; meatless Western vegetable soup, 105–6; sauerkraut, 107; sour, 119

cake: angel food cake, 52–53; cinnamon kuchen, 120–21; instant angel food cake, 157–58; peach melba, 131; white, 14–15

cake frosting/icing: cooked mint, 157–58; sugar, 15

candied sweet potatoes, 85–86

candy: bittersweet chocolate-peppermint wafers, 61; cream pulled candy, 36–37; creamy chocolate fudge, 34; divinity, 33; modjeskas, 35; peanut brittle, 36; pecan pralines, 34–35; pudding, 32; sea foam, 32–33

Cape Cod clam chowder, 59–60

caramel sauce: 91; for ice cream, 145

carrots (lemon-glazed), 198–99

casserole: broccoli, 198; ham and scalloped potatoes, 152–53; scalloped oyster plant (salsify), 194–95; tomato okra casserole, 197–98

chan tart, 12–13

cheese: egg sausage casserole, 135; open-faced grilled sandwich, 92; pimiento spread, 64; straws, 78–79; Welsh rarebit, 138

chess pie, 205–6

chicken: a la king, 95; a la king pastry shells, 130; arroz con pollo, 27–28; breasts, 114–15; creamed mold, 94; croquettes, 95–96; cut up, 151; fried, 44–45; giblets, 115; hash, 154; legs and thighs, 115; pot pies, 153; salad, 181; Shakertown fried, 176; stock, 114

Chinese spareribs, 114

chocolate: chunk squares, 112; creamy fudge, 34; fudge pie, 149–50; hot cocoa with marshmallows, 133–34; hot fudge sauce, 88–89; Kentucky bourbon balls, 201–2; meringue pie, 149

cinnamon kuchen and topping, 120–21

coconut cream tarts, 199

coleslaw, 55–56

combination salad, 19–20

congealed salad, 178–79

cooked mint frosting, 157–58

cookies: crunchy peanut butter, 144; gingerbread boys, 111–12; icing for, 124; pfeffernuesse, 121–22; refrigerator, 144–45; shortbread (springerle), 122–23; "we don't like those cookies," 123–24

corn: fritters, 12; soup, 40; sticks, 206; stewed fried, 155

country: dressing, 180–81; gravy, 45; ham biscuits, 180; sausage, 9–10

crabmeat salad, 80–81
cranberry pineapple congealed salad, 87–88
cream: gravy, 18–19; mushroom sauce, 94; pulled candy, 36–37; sauce, 93–94
creamed: chicken mold, 94; chipped beef on toast, 54; eggs on baked potatoes or toast, 156; oysters, 11; peas and mushrooms, 86; spam and eggs, 109–10
creamy chocolate fudge, 34
crunchy peanut butter cookies, 144
cucumber: Benedictine spread, 65; sandwich, 43
custard for prune whip, 143

daiquiri, 77–78
deviled: eggs, 155; ham spread, 64
divinity, 33

egg(s): a la King, 94; aspic on anchovy toast, 170–71; creamed on baked potatoes or toast, 156; deviled, 155; kisses, 131–32; salad sandwiches, 137; sauce, 58; sausage and cheese casserole, 135
Elizabeth's instant angel food cake, 157–58

fish. See seafood
floating island prune whip, 142–43

French Village rolls, 71
fresh salmon loaf with egg sauce, 57–58
fried: apples, 174–75; chicken, 44–45; Shakertown fried, 176
frosting. See cake frosting/icing
fruit: hot curried, 173–74; salad and dressing, 28–29

gazpacho, 26–27
German potato salad, 117
ginger bread and brown sugar sauce, 46–47
gingerbread boys, 111–12
glaze for ham, 176
grape and mandarin orange salad, 129
grapefruit and avocado salad, 140
gravy: country, 45; cream, 18–19
griddle cakes, 177–78

ham. See pork
ham and scalloped potatoes, 152–53
ham salad, 152
hard sauce, 91–92
hash, 154
hot cocoa with marshmallows, 133–34
hot curried fruit, 173–74
hot fudge sauce, 88–89

icebox rolls, 17–18
iced potato soup, 190
icing. See cake frosting/icing
icing for cookies, 124

junket (vanilla rennet custard), 31

Kentucky: bourbon balls, 201–2; sugar pie, 90

lemon-glazed carrots, 198–99
lime drink, 29

marinated asparagus, 154
mayonnaise, 65–66
meat loaf, 84
meatless western vegetable soup, 105–6
meringue, 149
mint julep, 78
modjeskas, 35
muffins. *See* bread(s)
mush, 45
mushroom(s): cream sauce, 94; creamed chicken mold, 94; creamed peas, 86; eggs a la king, 93–94; spaghetti Italian, 141
mustard sauce, 60–61

navy bean soup, 110–11
night before buckwheat cakes, 7

oatmeal pie, 200
old recipe beaten biscuits, 21
olive nut spread, 64
onion soup, 66
open-faced grilled cheese sandwich, 92
orange marmalade, 9
oyster(s): creamed, 11; pan-fried, 141–42; Rockefeller, 82; stew, 81

pancakes, 7–8
pan-fried oysters, 141–42
Parker House rolls, 130–31
pastry shells, 130
peach melba, 131
peanut brittle, 36
pear and Roquefort cheese salad, 139
pecan(s): apricot cream cheese spread, 65; balls, 88–89; chicken salad, 180–81; chocolate chunk squares, 112; Kentucky bourbon balls, 201–2; olive nut spread, 64; pie, 90; pralines, 34–35; squash muffins, 172; "we don't like those cookies" cookies, 123–24
pfeffernuesse, 121–22
pickled pig's feet, 127
pie: chess, 205–6; chocolate meringue, 149; fudge, 149; Kentucky sugar, 90; oatmeal, 200; pecan, 90; pumpkin, 143–44; Shaker lemon, 167
piecrust: 89; cuttings with cinnamon sugar, 156
pimiento cheese spread, 64
Pleasant Hill salad plate with country ham biscuits and chicken salad, 178–79
pork: bacon buns, 135; baked ham with mustard sauce, 60–61; baked country ham, 175–76; baked spam with pineapple, 108; breaded

chops, 140–41; Chinese spareribs, 114; country sausage, 9–10; creamed spam with eggs, 109–10; ham and scalloped potatoes, 152–53; ham salad, 152; pickled pig's feet, 127; spam pancakes, 109; spareribs, 107–8
potato: chips, 37–38; German salad, 117; hash, 154; iced soup, 190; old-fashioned soup, 83; sour, 118
pot pies, 153
pot roast, 75
pumpkin pie, 143–44

quail (broiled), 18
quick cocktail sauce, 142

refrigerator cookies, 144–45
relish bowl, 187–88
ribbon sandwiches, 63–66
Rita's healthy complexion rice, 113–14
rolls: French Village, 71; icebox, 17–18; Parker House, 130–31; whole wheat, 185–86
Russian dressing, 16–17

salad: banana peanut butter, 87; chicken, 180–81; combination, 19–20; congealed, 178–79; crabmeat, 80–81; cranberry pineapple congealed, 87–88; fruit, 28–29; German potato, 117; grape and mandarin orange, 129; grapefruit and avocado, 140; ham, 152; pear and Roquefort cheese, 139; summer vegetable molded, 106–7; victory garden, 106
salad dressing: Anna's French, 140; boiled, 56; fruit, 28–29; Russian, 16–17
sandwiches: cucumber, 43; egg salad, 137; open-faced grilled cheese, 92; ribbon, 63–66; shrimp salad, 137–38
sauce: basic cream 93–94; basic white, 96–97, 155–56; brown sugar, 46; caramel, 91; caramel sauce for ice cream, 145; cocktail, 142; cream, 93–94; cream mushroom, 94; egg, 58; hard, 91–92; hot fudge, 88–89; mustard, 60–61
sauerkraut, 107
scalloped oyster plant (salsify), 194–95
schmierkase, 118–19
sea foam, 32–33
seafood: baked fish, 27; Cape Cod clam chowder, 59–60; crabmeat salad, 80–81; creamed oysters, 11; oyster stew, 81; oysters Rockefeller, 82; pan-fried oysters, 141–42; salmon loaf, 57–58; shrimp salad sandwiches, 137–38; soft-shell crab, 80
Shaker lemon pie, 167
Shakertown fried chicken, 176
shrimp salad sandwiches, 137–38

soft-shell crab, 80
soup(s): baked bean, 83–84; Cape
    Cod clam chowder, 59–60;
    corn, 40; gazpacho, 26–27;
    iced potato, 190; navy bean,
    110–11; old-fashioned potato,
    83; onion, 66; split pea,
    125–26; tomato celery, 188–
    89; vegetable, 152, 189–90;
    western vegetable, 105–6
sour: cabbage, 119; potatoes, 118
spaghetti Italian, 141
Spam pancakes, 109
Spanish rice, 110
spareribs and sauerkraut, 107–8
spiced tea, 42
split pea soup, 125–26
spread(s): apricot cream
    cheese, 65; Benedictine, 65;
    deviled ham, 64; olive nut,
    64; pimiento cheese, 64;
    schmierkase, 118–19
springerle, 122–23
squash muffins, 172
stewed fried corn, 155
Stewed rhubarb, 86–87
stuffed peppers, 19
sugar icing, 15

sugar pie (Kentucky), 90
summer vegetable molded salad,
    106–7
Swiss steak, 85

tart(s): chan, 12–13; coconut
    cream, 199
tomato: aspic, 129–30; celery
    soup, 188–89; gazpacho,
    26–27; okra casserole, 197–98;
    open-faced grilled cheese
    sandwich, 92; spaghetti
    Italian, 141; Swiss steak, 85
turkey hash griddle cakes, 177–78

vanilla rennet custard (junket), 31
vegetable soup, 152, 189–90
victory garden salad, 106

"we don't like those cookies"
    cookies, 123–24
Welsh rarebit, 138
western vegetable soup, 105–6
we three ice, 43
white cake, 14–15
white sauce (basic), 96–97,
    155–56
whole wheat rolls, 185–86